Workshop on Constraints and Language Processing 2006

(CSLP 06)

Held in conjunction with COLING/ACL 2006

Sydney, Australia
22 July 2006

ISBN: 978-1-61738-499-8

Printed from e-media with permission by:

Curran Associates, Inc.
57 Morehouse Lane
Red Hook, NY 12571
www.proceedings.com

Some format issues inherent in the e-media version may also appear in this print version.

Printed by Curran Associates, Inc. (2010)

Association for Computational Linguistics
209 N. Eighth Street
Stroudsburg, Pennsylvania 18360

Phone: 1-570-476-8006
Fax: 1-570-476-0860

acl@aclweb.org

Table of Contents

Preface

The CSLP workshops address the question of constraints and their use in language processing. This is a characteristically interdisciplinary topic, bringing together perspectives from linguistics, psychology and computer science.

The 2 previous meetings, CSLP-04 in Roskilde (Denmark) and CSLP-05 in Sitges (Spain), focused more specifically on the question of constraint solving. For this meeting, we decided to broaden the perspective and encourage submissions from other domains. This aspect is quite a success: you will find in these proceedings papers in linguistics, psycholinguistics and natural language processing, all of them approaching the notion of constraint from different point of views. Moreover, our invited speaker this year, Prof. Edward Gibson (MIT, USA), also contributed to the enrichment of the perspective.

I would like to warmly thank all the PC members for their great job during the selection process. I also thank Henning Christiansen for having implemented over the past two years the idea of CSLP and Veronica Dahl for her support. Last, but not least, I deeply thank Jean-Philippe Prost for his help, especially during the proceedings editing process.

The Laboratoire Parole et Langage is the main sponsor for CSLP-06.

Philippe Blache
CSLP-06 Chair

Organizers

Chair:

Philippe Blache, Université de Provence, France

Other Organizers:

Henning Christiansen, Roskilde University, Denmark
Veronica Dahl, Simon Fraser University, Canada
Jean-Philippe Prost, Macquarie University, Australia, and Université de Provence, France

Program Committee:

Timothy Baldwin, University of Melbourne, Australia
Philippe Blache (Chair), Université de Provence, France
Henning Christiansen, Roskilde University, Denmark
Veronica Dahl, Simon Fraser University, Canada
Rina Dechter, University of California at Irvine, USA
Mark Dras, Macquarie University, Australia
Denys Duchier, Université d'Orléans, France
John Gallagher, Roskilde University, Denmark
Claire Gardent, Loria, France
Edward Gibson, MIT, USA
Mary Harper, Purdue University, USA
Barbara Hemforth, Université de Provence, France
Erhard Hinrichs, Universität Tübingen, Germany
Jerry Hobbs, University of Southern California, USA
Michael Johnston, ATT, USA
Tibor Kiss, Ruhr-Universität Bochum, Germany
Lars Konieczny, Universität Freiburg, Germany
Shalom Lappin, King's College, UK
Detmar Meurers, Ohio State University, USA
Joachim Niehren, INRIA, France
Gerald Penn, University of Toronto, Canada
Geoffrey Pullum, University of California Santa Cruz, USA
Ivan Sag, Stanford University, USA
Kiril Simov, Bulgarian Academy of Sciences, Bulgaria
Peter Skadhauge, Copenhagen Business School, Denmark
Gert Smolka, Universität des Saarlandes, Germany
Jorgen Villadsen, Roskilde University, Denmark
Eric Villemonte de la Clergerie, INRIA, France

Invited Speaker:

Edward Gibson, MIT, USA

Workshop Program

Saturday, 22 July 2006

8:45–9:00 Opening Remarks

9:00–10:30 Invited Talk by Edward Gibson

10:30–11:00 Coffee break

Session: Constraints and Language Processing

11:00–11:45 *Constraints in Language Processing: Do Grammars Count?*
Marieke van der Feen, Petra Hendriks and John Hoeks

11:45–12:30 *Control Strategies for Parsing with Freer Word-Order Languages*
Gerald Penn, Stefan Banjevic and Michael Demko

12:30–14:00 Lunch

14:00–14:45 *Numbat: Abolishing Privileges when Licensing New Constituents in Constraint-Oriented Parsing*
Jean-Philippe Prost

14:45–15:30 *Pragmatic Constraints on Semantic Presupposition*
Yafa Al-Raheb

15:30–16:00 Coffee break

16:00–16:45 *Coupling a Linguistic Formalism and a Script Language*
Claude Roux

16:45–17:30 *Capturing Disjunction in Lexicalization with Extensible Dependency Grammar*
Jorge Marques Pelizzoni and Maria das Graças Volpe Nunes

Constraints in Language Processing: Do Grammars Count?

Marieke van der Feen
Department of Artificial Intelligence,
University of Groningen,
Grote Kruisstraat 2/1,
9712 TS Groningen,
The Netherlands
mvdfeen@ai.rug.nl

Petra Hendriks
Center for Language and Cognition Groningen,
University of Groningen,
P.O. Box 716,
9700 AS Groningen,
The Netherlands
p.hendriks@rug.nl

John Hoeks
Center for Language and Cognition Groningen,
University of Groningen
P.O. Box 716,
9700 AS Groningen,
The Netherlands
j.c.j.hoeks@rug.nl

Abstract

One of the central assumptions of Optimality Theory is the hypothesis of strict domination among constraints. A few studies have suggested that this hypothesis is too strong and should be abandoned in favor of a weaker cumulativity hypothesis. If this suggestion is correct, we should be able to find evidence for cumulativity in the comprehension of Gapping sentences, which lack explicit syntactic clues in the form of the presence of a finite verb. On the basis of a comparison between several computational models of constraint evaluation, we conclude that the comprehension of Gapping sentences does not yield compelling evidence against the strict domination hypothesis.

1 Introduction

A linguistic framework which has gained a considerable amount of attention in recent years is Optimality Theory (Prince and Smolensky, 1993/2004). Optimality Theory (henceforth OT) is not only used for analyzing and explaining linguistic phenomena in the domain of phonology, but also in the domains of morphology, syntax, semantics and pragmatics. In contrast to more traditional linguistic frameworks, OT assumes grammatical constraints to be violable. Because constraints are formulated in such a way that they are maximally general (and perhaps even universal across languages), these constraints may conflict. To resolve conflicts among constraints, constraints are assumed to differ in strength. It is better to violate a weaker constraint than it is to violate a stronger constraint. The grammatical structure is the one that violates the least highly ranked (i.e., strong) constraints.

A fundamental property of OT is the principle of strict domination. This means that each constraint has complete priority over all constraints ranked lower in the constraint hierarchy. A number of recent studies, however, have called into question this fundamental property of OT. Keller (2001) argues that constraint violations must be cumulative to account for the pattern of relative acceptability with respect to the phenomenon of Gapping. Jäger and Rosenbach (to appear) draw a similar conclusion on the basis of the observed variation with respect to the English genitive (*the king's palace* versus *the palace of the king*).

In this study, we focus on the linguistic phenomenon of Gapping. The central question is whether the comprehension of Gapping sentences provides evidence in favor of cumulativity of constraint violations. In section 2, we introduce the phenomenon and discuss the possibility of an OT model of Gapping. In section 3, we consider different kinds of cumulativity. Section 4 discusses the way we modeled four different evaluation algorithms based on these kinds of cumulativity. A comparison between our computational models of constraint evaluation in section 5 suggests that the comprehension of Gapping does not provide compelling evidence for abandoning the strict domination hypothesis.

2 Gapping

Gapping is a grammatical operation that deletes certain subconstituents in the second conjunct of a coordinate structure, as in (1):

Proceedings of the 3rd Workshop on Constraints and Language Processing (CSLP-06), pages 1–8,
Sydney, July 2006. ©2006 Association for Computational Linguistics

(1) Some ate beans, and others rice.

The deleted material always includes the finite verb, but may also include further constituents such as the direct object. As a result, it may not always be possible to uniquely identify which elements were left out. As an example, consider the following sentence:

(2) John greeted Paul yesterday and George today.

This sentence is ambiguous between reading (3), where first John greeted Paul, and then John greeted George, and reading (4), where first John greeted Paul, and then George greeted Paul.

(3) John greeted Paul yesterday and ~~John greeted~~ George today.
(4) John greeted Paul yesterday and George ~~greeted Paul~~ today.

The reading in (3) is traditionally analyzed as resulting from the operation of conjunction reduction, whereas the reading in (4) is analyzed as resulting from Gapping of the finite verb and the direct object.

2.1 Functional constraints on Gapping

Based on previous work on Gapping, Kuno (1976) notes that several non-syntactic factors affect the acceptability and interpretation of Gapping. One of these factors is the distance between the remnants in the second conjunct and their counterparts in the first conjunct:

(5) *The Minimal Distance Principle:*
The two constituents left behind by Gapping can be most readily coupled with the constituents (of the same structures) in the first conjunct that were processed last of all.

According to this principle, interpretation (3) should be preferred for sentence (2) because it is more preferable to couple *George* in the second conjunct to the direct object *Paul* in the first conjunct, than to the more distant subject *John*. This preference is confirmed by experimental evidence (Carlson, 2001). A further principle about Gapping is that the deleted material has to represent contextually given information, whereas the remnants in the second conjunct have to constitute new information. This is captured in the following principle:

(6) *The Functional Sentence Perspective (FSP) Principle of Gapping:*
a. Constituents deleted by Gapping must be contextually known. On the other hand, the two constituents left behind by Gapping necessarily represent new information and, therefore, must be paired with constituents in the first conjunct that represent new information.
b. It is generally the case that the closer a given constituent is to sentence-final position, the newer the information it represents in the sentence.
c. Constituents that are clearly marked for nonanaphoricity necessarily represent new information in violation of (b). Similarly, constituents that appear closest tot sentence-final position necessarily represent old information (in violation of (b)) if coreferential constituents appear in the corresponding position in the preceding discourse.

This principle explains the observation that in a suitable context, interpretation (4) can become the preferred interpretation for (2) (but see Hoeks et al. (2006) for experimental evidence that in addition to context also prosody has to be in accordance with a Gapping reading to make this reading the preferred reading):

(7) When did John and George greet Paul?
John greeted Paul yesterday and George ~~greeted Paul~~ today.

In this example, John, Paul and George are all contextually introduced. But only John and George are subjects in the context sentence and hence can be interpreted as contrastive topics in the target sentence. Contrast has a similar effect as newness. Because of this effect of context, the Gapping reading can become the preferred reading for (2). Two further principles proposed by Kuno are (8) and (9).

(8) *The Tendency for Subject-Predicate Interpretation:*
When Gapping leaves an NP and a VP behind, the two constituents are readily interpreted as constituting a sentential pattern, with the NP representing the subject of the VP.

(9) *The Requirement for Simplex-Sentential Relationship:*
The two constituents left over by Gapping are most readily interpretable as entering into a simplex-sentential relationship. The intelligibility of gapped sentences declines drastically if there is no such relationship between the two constituents.

The principle in (8) is meant to account for a difference in preference with object control verbs versus subject control verbs. The principle in (9) reflects the observation that Gapping cannot leave behind remnants that are part of a subordinate clause. Kuno notes that this latter constraint seems to be the strongest of the four principles, being nearly inviolable, but does not make the interaction between his principles explicit.

2.2 An OT model of Gapping

As Kuno already observes, the FSP Principle seems to be able to override the Minimal Distance Principle. This observation is regarded by Keller (2001) as evidence that Gapping is subject to constraint competition in an optimality theoretic sense. Based on Kuno's principles, Keller develops an OT model of Gapping, which is able to account for the pattern of relative acceptability of Gapping sentences. According to this model, the degree of acceptability of a candidate structure depends on the number and type of rerankings required to make the structure optimal (Keller, 1998).

Keller's OT model differs from standard OT in a number of ways. Firstly, a distinction is made between soft and hard constraints. Hard constraints cause strong acceptability when violated, while violation of soft constraints causes only mild unacceptability. According to Keller, the Requirement for Simplex-Sentential Relationship is such a hard constraint. The distinction between soft and hard constraints is needed in Keller's model to avoid the problem of overgeneration of acceptability differences.

Secondly, Keller's model assumes that constraint violations are cumulative. According to his model, the degree of unacceptability increases with the number of constraints violated. In standard OT, on the other hand, no number of violations of weaker constraints can override one violation of a stronger constraint, in accordance with the principle of strict domination.

The aim of Keller's OT model is to account for the pattern of relative acceptability of Gapping sentences. The aim of the present study, on the other hand, is to account for the comprehension of Gapping sentences. Nevertheless, we follow Keller in adopting Kuno's functional principles (reformulated as OT constraints) for our OT model because Kuno's principles are principles of comprehension.

Our model differs from Keller's model in several essential aspects, though. We assume that all constraints are violable, in accordance with the basic assumptions of OT. Because certain strong constraints are not violated by the data under discussion, they simply appear to be inviolable. Keller's second assumption, the assumption that constraint violations are cumulative, is the topic of investigation of this study.

3 Cumulativity of constraint violations

In this section we discuss the different ways OT constraints can interact. In principle, OT constraints can interact in an unrestricted way, or in one of several more or less restricted ways.

3.1 Unrestricted constraint interaction

OT as a linguistic theory is derived from Harmonic Grammar (Legendre et al., 1990). In Harmonic Grammar (henceforth HG), each constraint is associated with a positive or negative numerical weight value. For each candidate, a so-called Harmony value is calculated by summing the numerically weighted constraints. From the set of candidates, the candidate with the highest Harmony value is selected as the optimal candidate. Consequently, the interaction among constraints in HG is cumulative. Each constraint violation lowers the Harmony value of the candidate. This type of constraint interaction is essentially unrestricted.

To account for natural language interpretation, however, unrestricted cumulativity is too liberal, as is shown by OT analyses of other phenomena. With respect to Gapping, if Kuno and Keller are right, no amount of violations on weaker constraints of an interpretation satisfying Simplex-Sentential Relationship can make an interpretation violating Simplex-Sentential Relationship the preferred one:

(10) Who did John promise to examine who?
John promised Paul to examine George, and Ringo Bob.

If Simplex-Sentential Relationship indeed is a strong constraint, (10) should only mean that

Ringo promised to examine Bob (satisfying Simplex-Sentential Relationship but violating the Minimal Distance Principle and the FSP), and never that John promised to examine Bob (violating Simplex-Sentential Relationship).

For the analysis of natural language, therefore, but also for the establishment of cross-linguistic generalizations (see Legendre et al., 2006), we seem to require a type of constraint interaction which is more restricted than simple numerical constraint weighting.

3.2 Restricted constraint interaction

In this section we discuss four ways to restrict constraint interaction: (1) strict domination, (2) local restricted cumulativity, (3) global restricted cumulativity, and (4) Keller's counting cumulativity.

	A	B	C	D
☞ Candidate 1		*	*	*
Candidate 2	*!			

Tableau 1: Strict domination

Strict domination is illustrated in tableau 1. The constraints are ordered from left to right in the top row in order of descending strength. Under strict domination, no number of violations of the weaker constraints B, C and D is able to override a violation of the strongest constraint A.

	A	B	C	D
Candidate 1			*!	*!
☞ Candidate 2		*		

Tableau 2: Local restricted cumulativity

Tableau 2 illustrates local restricted cumulativity. When the weaker constraints C and D are simultaneously violated, their joint effect can be stronger than their linear sum. As a result, together they are able to override the immediately dominating constraint B. This type of cumulativity is similar to the effects of local conjunction. The result is a conjoined constraint C&D, which is ranked immediately above constraint B in the hierarchy.

	A	B	C	D
Candidate 1			*!	*!
☞ Candidate 2	*			

Tableau 3: Global restricted cumulativity

An illustration of global restricted cumulativity is given in tableau 3. In this case, the weaker constraints C and D together are able to override a stronger, but not necessarily immediately dominating, constraint A. Again, this type of cumulativity is similar to the effects of local conjunction. The result is a conjoined constraint C&D, which is ranked anywhere above C and D in the hierarchy.

	A	B	C	D
Candidate 1		*	*!	*
☞ Candidate 2	*			

Tableau 4: Keller's counting cumulativity

Keller's counting cumulativity is illustrated in tableau 4. For Keller's cumulativity, the hierarchical relation between the constraints is irrelevant. The candidate with the fewest constraint violations is always optimal. In Keller's model, constraint violations are assumed to result in a gradient pattern. The more constraints are violated by a given Gapping construction, the less acceptable the construction is predicted to be. Of course, this type of cumulativity will greatly overgenerate in production as well as in comprehension if every constraint violation counts as an equally serious violation. For this reason, a system employing this type of cumulativity must make a distinction between soft and hard constraints. Hard constraints cause strong unacceptability. This extra assumption serves to restrict the overgenerating power of this type of cumulativity.

The four types of cumulativity discussed here differ in the amount of freedom they allow. Strict domination is the most restricted type of constraint interaction, local restricted cumulativity the one but most restricted type, global restricted cumulativity the two but most restricted type, and Keller's cumulativity the least restricted type. As a result, strict domination yields the strongest hypothesis, and Keller's cumulativity the weakest hypothesis. The question we set out to answer in the next section is how strongly constraint interaction must be restricted to account for the comprehension of Gapping sentences.

4 Testing the evaluation algorithms

To test the predictions of the four types of cumulativity discussed in the previous section, a computer model was developed in Prolog. The input to the model is a Gapping sentence in Dutch. The first conjunct is manually parsed. Information about the givenness of its constituents, the selectional restrictions of the main verb of the first conjunct, and featural information for all NPs is added. The output of the model is formed by the possible couplings of constituents in the second conjunct with constituents in the first conjunct. In addition, for each possible coupling the constraint profile is given. For each possible coupling, the model also gives a reconstruction of the second conjunct by placing the constituents from the second conjunct in the position of the constituents they are coupled with in the first conjunct.

4.1 Constraint ranking

The constraints implemented in the model were Kuno's principles, reformulated as OT constraints, augmented with constraints on parallelism (cf. Carlson, 2001), thematic selection (Hoeks and Hendriks, 2005) and word order (Lamers and de Hoop, 2004). The constraint ranking used is:

(11) Categorial Parallelism >> Simplex-Sentential Relationship >> FSP >> Thematic Selection >> Subject Precedes Object >> Syntactic Parallelism >> Minimal Distance >> Subject-Predicate Interpretation >> Featural Parallelism

The constraint Categorial Parallelism is added to ensure that constituents are coupled with constituents of the same syntactic category only. It prevents, for example, that in (2) *today* is coupled with *Paul*. Thematic Selection expresses the selectional restrictions verbs may impose on their arguments. For example, the verb *bake* requires an inanimate object, the verb *introduce* requires an animate object, and the verb *take* can combine with either an animate or an inanimate object (see section 4.3). The constraint Thematic Selection is violated if the candidate interpretation does not satisfy these selectional restrictions, for example if the object of the verb *bake* is animate. According to the constraint Subject Precedes Object, the subject must linearly precede the object. Syntactic Parallelism requires the two conjuncts to have the same syntactic structure. The constraint Featural Parallelism, finally, promotes the coupling of constituents which share features such as animacy, definiteness, number and gender. The ranking of these constraints was determined on the basis of the literature (Carlson, 2001; Kuno, 1976) and via comparison of relevant sentences and their meanings.

4.2 Computational considerations

The different types of cumulativity were computationally modeled as different ways of evaluating the constraint profiles.

Strict domination can be modeled as numerical weighting with exponential weights.

Local restricted cumulativity can be modeled as numerical weighting as well, if the weights are chosen in such a way that the sum of two adjacent constraints is larger than the weight of the directly dominating constraint. This is the case if, for example, B is 0.50, C is 0.26, and D is 0.25 in tableau 2. In our model, local restricted cumulativity only applies to the constraints Thematic Selection, Subject Precedes Object and Syntactic Parallelism, and allows the constraints Subject Precedes Object and Syntactic Parallelism together to override the directly dominating constraint Thematic Selection.

Global restricted cumulativity, on the other hand, cannot be captured straightforwardly in a system with weight values. To implement this evaluation method, therefore, we made explicit use of constraint conjunction. The newly formed conjoined constraint C&D was located in the hierarchy somewhere above its constituting constraints C and D. Because violation of this conjoined constraint is dependent on the violation of each of the constituting constraints, the new constraint can only be evaluated in a second round of evaluation after all other constraints have been evaluated. This is an unfortunate complication of our implementation. Legendre et al. (2006: 352) show that this type of cumulativity can be implemented with weight values if constraint conjunction is assumed to involve a superlinear combination of weights (through summation as well as multiplication). In our model, only the constraints Minimal Distance and Subject-Predicate Interpretation were allowed to conjoin. The resulting conjoined constraint was located above Categorial Parallelism in the hierarchy.

For the fourth method of evaluation, Keller's counting cumulativity, simply counting the number of constraint violations suffices. By applying one of these four evaluation algorithms, the computational model yields an optimal interpretation for each combination of input and evaluation algorithm.

4.3 Input sentences

To test the four evaluation algorithms, we fed the model three types of input: (i) 10 Gapping sentences taken from a corpus, (ii) test sentences taken from all five conditions of Carlson's (2001) study on Gapping, and (iii) 15 handcrafted sentences.

The Eindhoven corpus (uit den Boogaart, 1975) is an annotated corpus of Dutch written text of about 750 000 words. We scanned the corpus for suitable Gapping sentences, which had to occur unembedded, contain an overt conjunction, and should not involve other deletion operations as well. Unfortunately, we only found 10 such Gapping sentences in the corpus, presumably because Gapping is quite rare. For all ten sentences, all evaluation methods produced the same outputs. Nine out of the ten optimal interpretations did not violate any of the constraints. One sentence involved a constraint violation by all models, namely a violation of the constraint Featural Parallelism:

(12) Groep 1 trok de arm na vijftien minuten uit de testkamer, en groep 4 na een uur.
Group 1 pulled the arm after fifteen minutes from the test room and group 4 after an hour.

The most plausible interpretation of this sentence is the interpretation that group 4 pulled the arm from the test room after an hour. The interpretation selected by all evaluation methods, however, was that group 1 pulled group 4 from the test room after an hour, thus satisfying Minimal Distance but violating Featural Parallelism. It may be that the strong parallelism between *group 1* and *group 4* sets up a contrast which evokes the constraint FSP even in the absence of an explicit linguistic context. If this is true, Minimal Distance must be violated in order to satisfy FSP.

We also fed the models test sentences taken from Carlson's (2001) written questionnaire. Carlson studied the interaction between Thematic Selection, Featural Parallelism and Minimal Distance by varying verb type (see the discussion of Thematic Selection in section 4.1) and properties of the noun phrases. She distinguished five conditions: the Bake A condition (*Alice bakes cakes for tourists and Caroline for her family*), the Bake B condition (*Alice bakes cakes for tourists and brownies for her family*), the Take A condition (*Josh visited the office during the vacation and Sarah during the week*), the Take B condition (*Josh visited Marjorie during the vacation and Sarah during the week*) and the Introduce condition (*Dan amazed the judges with his talent and James with his musicality*).

The four evaluation algorithms behaved exactly the same on all five conditions of Carlson because none of Carlson's sentences involves a simultaneous violation of Subject Precedes Object and Syntactic Parallelism (which would give rise to local restricted cumulativity in our model) or a simultaneous violation of Minimal Distance and Subject-Predicate Interpretation (which would give rise to global restricted cumulativity in our model). As a result, all models yielded a 100% Gapping response for Carlson's Bake A condition (compared to Carlson's subjects 81%) because for all models a violation of Thematic Selection is more serious than a violation of Minimal Distance. Furthermore, all models yielded a 100% non-Gapping response for her Bake B condition (compared to Carlson's subjects 97%) because a Gapping response violates Thematic Selection, Minimal Distance and Featural Parallelism whereas a non-Gapping response satisfies all three constraints. Finally, all models yielded a 100% non-Gapping response for Carlson's Take A condition (compared to Carlson's subjects 60%), her Take B condition (compared to Carlson's subjects 96%) and her Introduce condition (compared to Carlson's subjects 79%) because for all models a violation of Minimal Distance is more serious than a violation of Featural Parallelism, given the constraint ranking in (11).

So all models correctly predicted the interpretational preferences found in Carlson's experiment. However, subjects' percentages of non-Gapping responses on the Take A, Take B and Introduce condition varied considerably. This variation seems to be due to differences between the features of the NPs involved. In particular, in the Take A condition the feature animacy played a role, which seems to have a stronger effect than the other grammatical features that were manipulated. However, our constraint Featural Parallelism does not distinguish between animacy and other grammatical features. Moreover, our OT model is unable to capture the gradience that seems to result from the interaction between features.

4.4 Generating different predictions

Because the four evaluation algorithms behaved identically on all sentences taken from the corpus as well as on all sentences types from Carlson's study, we had to construct sentences on the basis of expected constraint violations in order to generate different predictions for the four evaluation algorithms. The following sentence is predicted to distinguish between strict domination and local restricted cumulativity:

(13) John picked a rose, and a tulip Paul.

If hearers interpret this sentence as meaning that a tulip picked Paul, they will have violated the stronger constraint Thematic Selection in order to satisfy the two weaker constraints Subject Precedes Object and Syntactic Parallelism. This then would constitute evidence for local restricted cumulativity. If, on the other hand, hearers interpret this sentence as meaning that Paul picked a tulip, then this is evidence for strict domination. Sentence (14) distinguishes between strict domination and global restricted cumulativity:

(14) John asked him to get Paul, and George to bring Ringo.

Because *him* is a pronoun, it counts as given for evaluating the constraint FSP. If hearers interpret this sentence as meaning that John asked George to bring Ringo, they will have violated the stronger constraint FSP in order to satisfy the weaker constraints Minimal Distance and Subject-Predicate Interpretation. Because FSP does not immediately dominate the weaker constraints, this would be evidence for global restricted cumulativity. To distinguish between strict domination and Keller's counting cumulativity, consider the following sentence:

(15) The children promised John to stop, and the neighbors to continue.

If hearers interpret this sentence as meaning that the neighbors promised John to continue, they violate the single stronger constraint Minimal Distance in favor of satisfaction of the two weaker constraints Subject-Predicate Interpretation and Featural Parallelism. Because these constraints would all be considered soft constraints according to Keller's distinction between hard and soft constraints, Keller's counting cumulativity predicts that this interpretation is preferred. The strict domination hypothesis, on the other hand, predicts that the interpretation is preferred according to which the children promised the neighbors to continue, since it is more important to satisfy the stronger constraint Minimal Distance than any number of weaker constraints.

5 Results and discussion

For all Gapping sentences occurring in the Eindhoven corpus and all Gapping sentences taken from the written part of Carlson's psycholinguistic study, the four evaluation algorithms yielded identical results. These sentences therefore do not shed any light on the central question of this study, namely whether the strict domination hypothesis should be abandoned in favor of a weaker cumulativity hypothesis.

To determine which evaluation algorithm models the way comprehenders process language best, we must look at the interpretations of sentences such as (13), (14) and (15). We presented 10 participants with a written questionnaire, which included 15 sentences distinguishing between the four evaluation algorithms. The reader is referred to van der Feen (2005) for the complete list of sentences. The results show that there does not seem to be a clear preference in interpretation for sentences such as (13), leaving the distinction between strict domination and local restricted cumulativity undecided. For sentences such as (14), on the other hand, there seems to be a clear preference for the reading supported by global restricted cumulativity. Sentences such as (15), finally, show no effects at all of Keller's counting cumulativity. For only one sentence only one subject preferred the interpretation according to which the neighbors promised John to continue, which favors the strict domination hypothesis and goes against Keller's cumulativity algorithm. This suggests that constraints on comprehension may be different from the principles governing acceptability judgments. Boersma (2004) argues that the paralinguistic task of providing acceptability judgments involves comprehension, but under a reverse mapping between meaning and form. An alternative view is that acceptability judgments involve a mapping from the given form to its optimal meaning ('what do I think the sentence means?'), followed by a mapping from that meaning to the optimal form for that meaning ('how would I express that meaning?'), thus involving principles of comprehension as well as production.

To conclude, there seems to be a slight indication of global restricted cumulativity in the comprehension of Gapping, but further study with a larger pool of subjects is required to confirm these initial findings.

However, a few remarks are in place here. First, note that for hearers to prefer the interpretation that Paul picked a tulip for (13), the hearer has to find some motivation in the linguistic context of the utterance for why the speaker chose to put the object first. In the absence of such a context supporting a non-canonical word order, the reading that Paul picked a tulip might be dispreferred anyway.

Also in sentence (14), context seems to play a crucial role. Although in general pronouns may be used to refer to given material, in certain contexts pronouns can be emphatically stressed. If the pronoun in (14) is stressed, it is much easier to couple *George* to *him* to obtain the reading that John asked George to bring Ringo. This effect of context and prosody may have been the main reason for the observed preferences.

6 Conclusion

A central principle of Optimality Theory is the hypothesis of strict domination among constraints. In this paper we investigated whether this hypothesis should be abandoned in favor of the weaker hypothesis that constraint violations are cumulative. Studying the effects of four different evaluation algorithms (three of which display some kind of cumulativity) on the comprehension of Gapping sentences, we found a slight indication of cumulativity effects. However, these effects are likely to disappear if the context and prosodic structure of the utterance are taken into account.

Acknowledgments

The authors thank three anonymous reviewers for their useful comments and suggestions. This research was funded by grant # 015.001.103 from NWO, awarded to Petra Hendriks.

References

Paul Boersma. 2004. *A stochastic OT account of paralinguistic tasks such as grammaticality and prototypicality judgments.* Unpublished manuscript, University of Amsterdam. Rutgers Optimality Archive #648.

Katy Carlson. 2001. The Effects of Parallelism and Prosody in the Processing of Gapping Structures. *Language and Speech*, 44(1):1-26.

John Hoeks, Petra Hendriks, and Louisa Zijlstra. 2006. The Predominance of Nonstructural Factors in the Processing of Gapping Sentences. In: R. Sun and N. Miyake (eds.), *Proceedings of the 28th Annual Conference of the Cognitive Science Society.*

John Hoeks, and Petra Hendriks. 2005. Optimality Theory and human sentence processing: The case of coordination. In: B.G. Bara, L. Barsalou, and M. Bucciarelli (eds.), *Proceedings of the 27th Annual Meeting of the Cognitive Science Society*, Erlbaum, Mahwah, NJ, pp. 959-964.

Gerhard Jäger, and Anette Rosenbach. To appear. The winner takes it all - almost. Cumulativity in grammatical variation. *Linguistics.*

Frank Keller. 1998. Gradient Grammaticality as an Effect of Selective Constraint Re-ranking. In: M.C. Gruber, D. Higgins, K.S. Olson, and T. Wysocki (eds.) *Papers from the 34th Meeting of the Chicago Linguistic Society.* Vol. 2: The Panels, Chicago, pp. 95-109.

Frank Keller. 2001. Experimental Evidence for Constraint Competition in Gapping Constructions. In: G. Müller and W. Sternefeld (eds.), *Competition in Syntax*, Mouton de Gruyter, Berlin, pp. 211-248.

Susumo Kuno. 1976. Gapping: A Functional Analysis. *Linguistic Inquiry*, 7:300-318.

Monique Lamers, and Helen de Hoop. 2004. The role of animacy information in human sentence processing captured in four conflicting constraints. In: H. Christiansen, P. Rossen Skadhauge, and J. Villadsen (eds.), *Constraint Solving and Language Processing.* Workshop proceedings, Roskilde Department of Computer Science, Roskilde University, pp. 102-113.

Géraldine Legendre, Yoshiro Miyata, and Paul Smolensky. 1990. Harmonic Grammar - A formal multi-level theory of linguistic well-formedness: An application. In: *Proceedings of the Twelfth Annual Conference of the Cognitive Science Society*, Erlbaum, Cambridge, MA, pp. 388-395.

Géraldine Legendre, Antonella Sorace, and Paul Smolensky. 2006. The Optimality Theory - Harmonic Grammar Connection. In: P. Smolensky and G. Legendre (eds.), *The Harmonic Mind*, Vol. 2, MIT Press, Cambridge, MA, pp. 339-402.

Alan Prince, and Paul Smolensky. 2004. *Optimality Theory: Constraint interaction in generative grammar.* Oxford, Blackwell. Previously distributed as Technical Report RuCCSTR-2, New Brunswick NJ, Rutgers Center for Cognitive Science, Rutgers University, 1993.

P.C. Uit den Boogaart. 1975. *Woordfrequenties in geschreven en gesproken Nederlands.* Werkgroep Frequentie-onderzoek van het Nederlands. Oosthoek, Scheltema & Holkema, Utrecht.

Marieke Van der Feen. 2005. *Do rules add up? A study of the application of Optimality Theory to the interpretation of gapping.* MSc Thesis Artificial Intelligence, University of Groningen.

Control Strategies for Parsing with Freer Word-Order Languages

Gerald Penn
Dept. of Computer Science
University of Toronto
Toronto M5S 3G4, Canada

Stefan Banjevic
Dept. of Mathematics
University of Toronto
Toronto M5S 2E4, Canada

Michael Demko
Dept. of Computer Science
University of Toronto
Toronto M5S 3G4, Canada

{gpenn,banjevic,mpademko}@cs.toronto.edu

Abstract

We provide two different methods for bounding search when parsing with freer word-order languages. Both of these can be thought of as exploiting alternative sources of constraints not commonly used in CFGs, in order to make up for the lack of more rigid word-order and the standard algorithms that use the assumption of rigid word-order implicitly. This work is preliminary in that it has not yet been evaluated on a large-scale grammar/corpus for a freer word-order language.

1 Introduction

This paper describes two contributions to the area of parsing over freer word-order (FWO) languages, i.e., languages that do not readily admit a semantically transparent context-free analysis, because of a looser connection between grammatical function assignment and linear constituent order than one finds in English. This is a particularly ripe area for constraint-based methods because such a large number of linguistic partial knowledge sources must be brought to bear on FWO parsing in order to restrict its search space to a size comparable to that of standard CFG-based parsing.

The first addresses the indexation of tabled substrings in generalized chart parsers for FWO languages. While chart parsing can famously be cast *as* deduction (Pereira and Warren, 1983), what chart parsing really *is* is an algebraic closure over the rules of a phrase structure grammar, which is most naturally expressed inside a constraint solver such as CHR (Morawietz, 2000). Ideally, we would like to use standard chart parsers for FWO languages, but because of the constituent ordering constraints that are implicit in the right-hand-sides (RHSs) of CFG rules, this is not possible without effectively converting a FWO grammar into a CFG by expanding its rule system exponentially into all possible RHS orders (Barton et al., 1987). FWO grammar rules generally cannot be used as they stand in a chart parser because tabled substrings record a non-terminal category C derived over a contiguous subspan of the input string from word i to word j. FWO languages have many phrasal categories that are not contiguous substrings.

Johnson (1985), Reape (1991) and others have suggested using bit vectors to index chart edges as an alternative to substring spans in the case of parsing over FWO languages, but that is really only half of the story. We still need a control strategy to tell us where we should be searching for some constituent at any point in a derivation. This paper provides such a control strategy, using this data structure, for doing search more effectively with a FWO grammar.

The second contribution addresses another source of constraints on the search space: the length of the input. While this number is not a constant across parses, it is constant within a single parse, and there are functions that can be precomputed for a fixed grammar which relate tight upper and lower bounds on the length of the input to both the height of a parse tree and other variables (defined below) whose values bound the recursion of the fixed phrase structure rule system. Iteratively computing and caching the values of these functions as needed allows us to invert them efficiently, and bound the depth of the search. This can be thought of as a partial substitute for the resource-bounded control that bottom-up parsing generally provides, Goal-directedness

Proceedings of the 3rd Workshop on Constraints and Language Processing (CSLP-06), pages 9–16,
Sydney, July 2006.

is maintained, because — with the use of constraint programming – it can still be used inside a top-down strategy. In principle, this could be worthwhile to compute for some CFGs as well, although the much larger search space covered by a naïve bottom-up parser in the case of FWO grammars (all possible subsequences, rather than all possible contiguous subsequences), makes it considerably more valuable in the present setting.

In the worst case, a binary-branching immediate dominance grammar (i.e., no linear precedence) could specify that every word belongs to the same category, W, and that phrases can be formed from every pair of words or phrases. A complete parsing chart in this case would have exponentially many edges, so nothing in this paper (or in the aforementioned work on bit vectors) actually improves the asymptotic complexity of the recognition task. Natural languages do not behave like this, however. In practice, one can expect more polymorphy in the part-of-speech/category system, more restrictions in the allowable combinations of words and phrases (specified in the immediate dominance components of a phrase structure rule system), and more restrictions in the allowable orders and discontinuities with which those argument categories can occur (specified in the linear precedence components of a phrase structure rule system).

These restrictions engender a system of constraints that, when considered as a whole, admit certain very useful, language-dependent strategies for resolving the (respectively, don't-care) nondeterministic choice points that a (resp., all-paths) parser must face, specifically: (1) which lexical categories to use (or, resp., in which order), given the input words, (2) which phrase structure rules to apply (resp., in which order), and (3) given a particular choice of phrase structure rule, in which order to search for the argument categories on its right-hand side (this one is don't-care nondeterministic even if the parser is looking for only the best/first parse). These heuristics are generally obtained either through the use of a parameter estimation method over a large amount of annotated data, or, in the case of a manually constructed grammar, simply through some implicit convention, such as the textual order in which the lexicon, rule system, or RHS categories are stated.[1]

This paper does not address how to find these heuristics. We assume that they exist, and instead address the problem of adapting a chart parser to their efficient use. To ignore this would involve conducting an enormous number of derivations, only to look in the chart at the end and discover that we have already derived the current bit-vector/category pair. In the case of standard CFG-based parsing, one generally avoids this by tabling so-called active edges, which record the subspaces on which a search has already been initiated. This works well because the only existentially quantified variables in the tabled entry are the interior nodes in the span which demarcate where one right-hand-side category ends and another adjacent one begins. To indicate that one is attempting to complete the rule, $S \rightarrow NP\ VP$, for example, one must only table the search from i to j for some k, such that NP is derivable from i to k and VP is derivable from k to j. Our first contribution can be thought of as a generalization of these active edges to the case of bit vectors.

2 FWO Parsing as Search within a Powerset Lattice

A standard chart-parser views constituents as extending over *spans*, contiguous intervals of a linear string. In FWO parsing, constituents partition the input into not necessarily contiguous subsequences, which can be thought of as bit vectors whose AND is 0 and whose OR is $2^n - 1$, given an initial n-length input string. For readability, and to avoid making an arbitrary choice as to whether the leftmost word should correspond to the most significant or least significant bit, we will refer to these constituents as subsets of $\{1 \ldots n\}$ rather than as n-length bit vectors. For simplicity and because of our heightened awareness of the importance of goal-directedness to FWO parsing (see the discussion in the previous section), we will only outline the strictly top-down variant of our strategy, although natural analogues do exist for the other orientations.

2.1 State

State is: $\langle N, \mathrm{CanBV}, \mathrm{ReqBV} \rangle$.
The returned result is: UsedBV **or failure.**

[1] In the case of the lexicon and rule system, there is a very long-standing tradition in logic programming of using this convention. To our knowledge, the first to apply it to the order of RHS categories, which only makes sense once one drops the implicit linear ordering implied by the RHSs of context-free grammar rules, was Daniels and Meurers (2002).

Following Penn and Haji-Abdolhosseini (2003), we can characterize a search state under these assumptions using one non-terminal, N, and two subsets/bit vectors, the *CanBV* and *ReqBV*.[2] CanBV is the set of all words that *can* be used to build an N, and ReqBV is the set of all words that *must* be used while building the N. CanBV always contains ReqBV, and what it additionally contains are optional words that may or may not be used. If search from this state is successful, i.e., N is found using ReqBV and nothing that is not in CanBV, then it returns a *UsedBV*, the subset of words that were actually used. We will assume here that our FWO grammars are not so free that one word can be used in the derivation of two or more sibling constituents, although there is clearly a generalization to this case.

2.2 Process

`Search`($\langle N, C, R\rangle$) can then be defined in the constraint solver as follows:

2.2.1 Initialization

A top-down parse of an n-length string begins with the state consisting of the distinguished category, S, of the grammar, and CanBV $=$ ReqBV $= \{1 \ldots n\}$.

2.2.2 Active Edge Subsumption

The first step is to check the current state against states that have already been considered. For expository reasons, this will be presented below. Let us assume for now that this step always fails to produce a matching edge. We must then predict using the rules of the FWO grammar.

2.2.3 Initial Prediction

$\langle N, C, R\rangle \Longrightarrow \langle N_1, C, \phi\rangle$, **where:**

1. $N_0 \rightarrow N_1 \ldots N_k$,
2. $k > 1$, **and**
3. $N \sqcup N_0\downarrow$.

As outlined in Penn and Haji-Abdolhosseini (2003), the predictive step from a state consisting of $\langle N, C, R\rangle$ using an immediate dominance rule, $N_0 \rightarrow N_1 \ldots N_k$, with $k > 1$ and no linear precedence constraints transits to a state $\langle N_1, C, \phi\rangle$ provided that N is compatible with N_0. In the case of a classical set of atomic non-terminals, compatibility should be interpreted as equality. In the case of Prolog terms, as in definite clause grammars, or typed feature structures, as in head-driven phrase structure grammar, compatibility can be interpreted as either unifiability or the asymmetric subsumption of N by N_0. Without loss of generality, we will assume unifiability here.

This initial predictive step says that there are, in general, no restrictions on which word must be consumed ($ReqBV = \phi$). Depending on the language chosen for expressing linear precedence restrictions, this set may be non-empty, and in fact, the definition of state used here may need to be generalized to something more complicated than a single set to express the required consumption constraints.

2.2.4 Subsequent Prediction

$\langle N, C, R\rangle \Longrightarrow \langle N_{j+1}, C_j, \phi\rangle$, **where:**

1. $N_0 \rightarrow N_1 \ldots N_k$,
2. $N \sqcup N_0\downarrow$,
3. $\langle N_1, C, \phi\rangle$ **succeeded with** U_1,

   ⋮

   $\langle N_j, C_{j-1}, \phi\rangle$ **succeeded with** U_j,
4. $k > 1$ and $1 \leq j < k - 1$, **and**
5. $C_j = C \cap \overline{U_1} \cap \ldots \cap \overline{U_j}$.

Regardless of these generalizations, however, each subsequent predictive step, having recognized $N_1 \ldots N_j$, for $1 \leq j < k-1$, computes the next CanBV C_j by removing the consumed words U_j from the previous CanBV C_{j-1}, and then transits to state $\langle N_{j+1}, C_j, \phi\rangle$. Removing the UsedBVs is the result of our assumption that no word can be used by two or more sibling constituents.

2.2.5 Completion

$\langle N, C, R\rangle \Longrightarrow \langle N_k, C_{k-1}, R_{k-1}\rangle$, **where:**

1. $N_0 \rightarrow N_1 \ldots N_k$,
2. $N \sqcup N_0\downarrow$,
3. $\langle N_1, C, \phi\rangle$ **succeeded with** U_1,

   ⋮

   $\langle N_{k-1}, C_{k-2}, \phi\rangle$ **succeeded with** U_{k-1},
4. $C_{k-1} = C \cap \overline{U_1} \cap \ldots \cap \overline{U}_{k-1}$, **and**
5. $R_{k-1} = R \cap \overline{U_1} \cap \ldots \cap \overline{U}_{k-1}$.

The completion step then involves recognizing the last RHS category (although this is no longer rightmost in terms of linear precedence). Here, the major difference from subsequent prediction is that there is now a potentially non-empty ReqBV. Only with the last RHS category are we actually in a position to enforce R from the source state.

If $\langle N_k, C_{k-1}, R_{k-1}\rangle$ succeeds with U_k, then $\langle N, C, R\rangle$ succeeds with $U_1 \cup \ldots \cup U_k$.

[2] Actually, Penn and Haji-Abdolhosseini (2003) use CanBV and *OptBV*, which can be defined as CanBV $\cap$ $\overline{\text{ReqBV}}$.

2.3 Active Edge Subsumption Revisited

So far, this is very similar to the strategy outlined in Penn and Haji-Abdolhosseini (2003). If we were to add active edges in a manner similar to standard chart parsing, we would tabulate states like $\langle N_a, C_a, R_a \rangle$ and then compare them in step 2.2.2 to current states $\langle N, C, R \rangle$ by determining whether (classically) $N = N_a$, $C = C_a$, and $R = R_a$. This might catch some redundant search, but just as we can do better in the case of non-atomic categories by checking for subsumption ($N_a \sqsubseteq N$) or unifiability ($N \sqcup N_a\downarrow$), we can do better on C and R as well because these are sets that come with a natural notion of containment.

Figure 1 shows an example of how this containment can be used. Rather than comparing edges annotated with linear subspans, as in the case of CFG chart parsing, here we are comparing edges annotated with sublattices of the powerset lattice on n elements, each of which has a top element (its CanBV) and a bottom element (its ReqBV). Everything in between this top and bottom is a subset of words that has been (or will be) tried if that combination has been tabled as an active edge.

Figure 1 assumes that $n = 6$, and that we have tabled an active edge (dashed lines) with $C_a = \{1, 2, 4, 5, 6\}$, and $R_a = \{1, 2\}$. Now suppose later that we decide to search for the same category in $C = \{1, 2, 3, 4, 5, 6\}$, $R = \{1, 2\}$ (dotted lines). Here, $C \neq C_a$, so an equality-based comparison would fail, but a better strategy would be to reallocate the one extra bit in C (3) to R, and then search $C' = \{1, 2, 3, 4, 5, 6\}$, $R' = \{1, 2, 3\}$ (solid lines). As shown in Figure 1, this solid region fills in all and only the region left unsearched by the active edge.

This is actually just one of five possible cases that can arise during the comparison. The complete algorithm is given in Figure 2. This algorithm works as a filter, which either blocks the current state from further exploration, allows it to be further explored, or breaks it into several other states that can be concurrently explored. Step 1(a) deals with category unifiability. If the current category, N, is unifiable with the tabled active category, N_a, then 1(a) breaks N into more specific pieces that are either incompatible with N_a or subsumed by N_a. By the time we get to 1(b), we know we are dealing with a piece that is subsumed by N_a. O stands for "optional," CanBV bits that are not required.

`Check`($\langle N, C, R \rangle$):

- For each active edge, a, with $\langle N_a, C_a, R_a \rangle$,
  1. If $N \sqcup N_a\downarrow$, then:
     (a) For each minimal category N' such that $N \sqsubseteq N'$ and $N' \sqcup N_a\uparrow$, concurrently:
        - Let $N := N'$, and continue [to next active edge].
     (b) Let $N := N \sqcup N_a$, $O := C \cap \overline{R}$ and $O_a := C_a \cap \overline{R_a}$.
     (c) If $C_a \cap \overline{O_a} \cap \overline{C} \neq \phi$, then continue [to next active edge].
     (d) If $C \cap \overline{O} \cap \overline{C_a} \neq \phi$, then continue [to next active edge].
     (e) If $(Z :=) O \cap \overline{C_a} \neq \phi$, then:
        i. Let $O := O \cap \overline{Z}$,
        ii. Concurrently:
           A. continue [to next active edge], and
           B. (1) Let $C := C \cap \overline{Z}$,
              (2) goto (1) [to reconsider this active edge].
     (f) If $(Z :=) C_a \cap \overline{O_a} \cap O \neq \phi$, then:
        i. Let $O := O \cap \overline{Z}$, $C := C \cap \overline{Z}$,
        ii. continue [to next active edge].
     (g) Fail — this state is subsumed by an active edge.
  2. else continue [to next active edge].

Figure 2: Active edge checking algorithm.

Only one of 1(g) or the bodies of 1(c), 1(d), 1(e) or 1(f) is ever executed in a single pass through the loop. These are the five cases that can arise during subset/bit vector comparison, and they must be tried in the order given. Viewing the current state's CanBV and ReqBV as a modification of the active edge's, the first four cases correspond to: the removal of required words (1(c)), the addition of required words (1(d)), the addition of optional (non-required) words (1(e)), and the reallocation of required words to optional words (1(f)). Unless one of these four cases has happened, the current sublattice has already been searched in its entirety (1(g)).

2.4 Linear Precedence Constraints

The elaboration above has assumed the absence of any linear precedence constraints. This is the

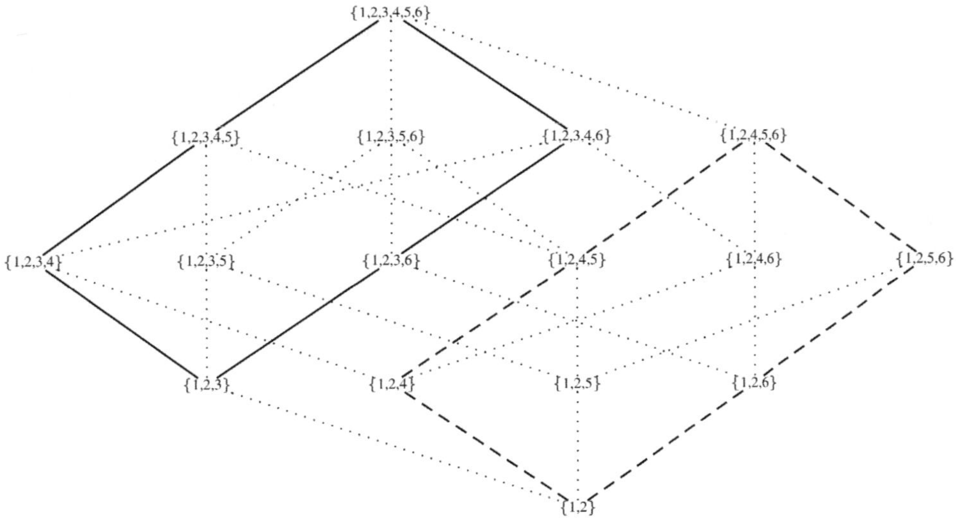

Figure 1: A powerset lattice representation of active edge checking with CanBV and ReqBV.

worst case, from a complexity perspective. The propagation rules of section 2.2 can remain unchanged in a concurrent constraint-based framework in which other linear precedence constraints observe the resulting algebraic closure and fail when violated, but it is possible to integrate these into the propagators for efficiency. In either case, the active edge subsumption procedure remains unchanged.

For lack of space, we do not consider the characterization of linear precedence constraints in terms of CanBV and ReqBV further here.

3 Category Graphs and Iteratively Computed Yields

Whereas in the last section we trivialized linear precedence, the constraints of this section simply do not use them. Given a FWO grammar, G, with immediate dominance rules, R, over a set of non-terminals, N, we define the *category graph* of G to be the smallest directed bipartite graph, $C(G) = \langle V, E\rangle$, such that:

- $V = N \cup R \cup \{\mathrm{Lex}, \mathrm{Empty}\}$,
- $(X, r) \in E$ if non-terminal X appears on the RHS of rule r,
- $(r, X) \in E$ if the LHS non-terminal of r is X,
- $(\mathrm{Lex}, r) \in E$ if there is a terminal on the RHS of rule r, and
- $(\mathrm{Empty}, r) \in E$ if r is an empty production rule.

We will call the vertices of $C(G)$ either *category nodes* or *rule nodes*. Lex and Empty are considered category nodes. The category graph of the grammar in Figure 3, for example, is shown in

S → VP NP	VP_1 → V NP
NP_1 → N' S	VP_2 → V
NP_2 → N'	N → {boy, girl}
N'_1 → N Det	Det → {a, the, this}
N'_2 → N	V → {sees, calls}

Figure 3: A sample CFG-like grammar.

Figure 4. By convention, we draw category nodes with circles, and rule nodes with boxes, and we label rule nodes by the LHS categories of the rules they correspond to plus an index. For brevity, we will assume a normal form for our grammars here, in which the RHS of every rule is either a string of non-terminals or a single terminal.

Category graphs are a minor variation of the "grammar graphs" of Moencke and Wilhelm (1982), but we will use them for a very different purpose. For brevity, we will consider only atomic non-terminals in the remainder of this section. Category graphs can be constructed for partially ordered sets of non-terminals, but in this case, they can only be used to approximate the values of the functions that they exactly compute in the atomic case.

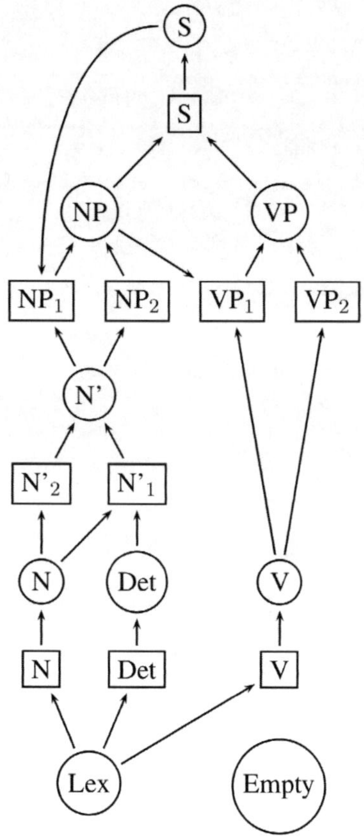

Figure 4: The category graph for the grammar in Figure 3.

Restricting search to unexplored sublattices helps us with recursion in a grammar in that it stops redundant search, but in some cases, recursion can be additionally bounded (above and below) not because it is redundant but because it cannot possibly yield a string as short or long as the current input string. Inputs are unbounded in size across parses, but within a single parse, the input is fixed to a constant size. Category graphs can be used to calculate bounds as a function of this size. We will refer below to the length of an input string below a particular non-terminal in a parse tree as the *yield* of that non-terminal instance. The *height* of a non-terminal instance in a parse tree is 1 if it is pre-terminal, and 1 plus the maximum height of any of its daughter non-terminals otherwise. Non-terminal categories can have a range of possible yields and heights.

3.1 Parse Tree Height

Given a non-terminal, X, let $X^{max}(h)$ be the maximum yield that a non-terminal instance of X at height h in any parse tree can produce, given the fixed grammar G. Likewise, let $X^{min}(h)$ be the minimum yield that such an instance must produce. Also, as an abuse of functional notation, let:

$$X^{max}(\leq h) = \max_{0\leq j\leq h} X^{max}(j)$$
$$X^{min}(\leq h) = \min_{0\leq j\leq h} X^{min}(j)$$

Now, using these, we can come back and define $X^{max}(h)$ and $X^{min}(h)$:

$$\text{Lex}^{max}(h) = $$
$$\text{Lex}^{min}(h) = \begin{cases} 1 & h=0 \\ \text{undefined} & \text{otherwise} \end{cases}$$
$$\text{Empty}^{max}(h) = $$
$$\text{Empty}^{min}(h) = \begin{cases} 0 & h=0 \\ \text{undefined} & \text{otherwise} \end{cases}$$

and for all other category nodes, X:

$$\text{X}^{max}(1) = $$
$$\text{X}^{min}(1) = \begin{cases} 0 & X \to \epsilon \in R \\ 1 & X \to t \in R \\ \text{undefined} & \text{otherwise} \end{cases}$$

and for $h > 1$:

$$X^{max}(h) = \max_{X\to X_1\ldots X_k\in R}\left(\max_{1\leq i\leq k} X_i^{max}(h-1) + \sum_{j=1,j\neq i}^{k} X_j^{max}(\leq h-1)\right)$$
$$X^{min}(h) = \min_{X\to X_1\ldots X_k\in R}\left(\min_{1\leq i\leq k} X_i^{min}(h-1) + \sum_{j=1,j\neq i}^{k} X_j^{min}(\leq h-1)\right).$$

For example, in Figure 3, there is only one rule with S as a LHS category, so:

$$\text{S}^{max}(h) = \max\begin{cases} \text{NP}^{max}(h-1) + \text{VP}^{max}(\leq h-1) \\ \text{NP}^{max}(\leq h-1) + \text{VP}^{max}(h-1) \end{cases}$$
$$\text{S}^{min}(h) = \min\begin{cases} \text{NP}^{min}(h-1) + \text{VP}^{min}(\leq h-1) \\ \text{NP}^{min}(\leq h-1) + \text{VP}^{min}(h-1). \end{cases}$$

These functions compute yields as a function of height. We know the yield, however, and want bounds on height. Given a grammar in which the non-pre-terminal rules have a constant branching factor, we also know that $X^{max}(h)$ and $X^{min}(h)$, are monotonically non-decreasing in h, where they are defined. This means that we can iteratively compute $X^{max}(h)$, for all non-terminals X, and all values h out to the first h' that produces a value strictly greater than the current yield (the length of the given input). Similarly, we can compute $X^{min}(h)$, for all non-terminals X, and all values h out to the first h'' that is equal to or greater than the current yield. The height of the resulting parse tree, h, can then be bounded as $h' - 1 \leq h \leq h''$. These iterative computations can be cached and reused across different inputs. In general, in the absence of a constant branching factor, we still have a finite maximum branching factor, from which an upper bound on any potential decrease in $X^{max}(h)$ and $X^{min}(h)$ can be determined.

This provides an interval constraint. Because there may be heights for which $X^{max}(h)$ and $X^{min}(h)$ is not defined, one could, with small enough intervals, additionally define a finite domain constraint that excludes these.

These recursive definitions are well-founded when there is at least one finite string derivable by every non-terminal in the grammar. The X^{min} functions converge in the presence of unit production cycles in $C(G)$; the X^{max} functions can also converge in this case. Convergence restricts our ability to constrain search with yields.

A proper empirical test of the efficacy of these constraints requires large-scale phrase structure grammars with weakened word-order constraints, which are very difficult to come by. On the other hand, our preliminary experiments with simple top-down parsing on the Penn Treebank II suggest that even in the case of classical context-free grammars, yield constraints can improve the efficiency of parsing. The latency of constraint enforcement has proven to be a real issue in this case (weaker bounds that are faster to enforce can produce better results), but the fact that yield constraints produce any benefit whatsoever with CFGs is very promising, since the search space is so much smaller than in the FWO case, and edge indexing is so much easier.

3.2 Cycle Variables

The heights of non-terminals from whose category nodes the cycles of $C(G)$ are not path-accessible can easily be bounded. Using the above height-dependent yield equations, the heights of the other non-terminals can also be bounded, because any input string fixes the yield to a finite value, and thus the height to a finite range (in the absence of converging X^{min} sequences). But we can do better. We can condition these bounds not only upon height but upon the individual rules used. We could even make them depend upon sequences of rules, or on vertical chains of non-terminals within trees. If $C(G)$ contains cycles, however, there are infinitely many such chains (although finitely many of any given length), but trips around cycles themselves can also be counted.

Let us formally specify that a *cycle* refers to a unique path from some category node to itself, such that every node along the path except the last is unique. Note that because $C(G)$ is bipartite, paths alternate between category nodes and rule nodes.

Now we can enumerate the distinct cycles of any category graph. In Figure 4, there are two, both passing through NP and S, with one passing through VP in addition. Note that cycles, even though they are unique, may share nodes as these two do. For each cycle, we will arbitrarily choose an *index node* for it, and call the unique edge along the cycle leading into that node its *index link*. It will be convenient to choose the distinguished non-terminal, S, as the index node when it appears in a cycle, and in other cases, to choose a node with a minimal path-distance to S in the category graph.

For each cycle, we will also assign it a unique *cycle variable* (written n, m etc.). The domain of this variable is the natural numbers and it counts the number of times in a parse that we traverse this cycle as we search top-down for a tree. When an index link is traversed, the corresponding cycle variable must be incremented.

For each category node X in $C(G)$, we can define the maximum and minimum yield as before, but now instead of height being the only independent parameter, we also make these functions depend on the cycle variables of all of the cycles that pass through X. If X has no cycles passing through it, then its only parameter is still h. We can also easily extend the definition of these functions to rule nodes.

Rather than provide the general definitions here, we simply give some of the equations for Figure 4, for shortage of space:

$$\mathrm{S}^{max}(h, n, m) = \mathrm{S}^{max}(h, \bar{n}, \bar{m})$$
$$\mathrm{S}^{max}(h, n, \bar{m}) = \mathrm{S}^{max}(h, \bar{n}, \bar{m})$$
$$\mathrm{S}^{max}(h, \bar{n}, \bar{m}) = \max_{\substack{i+j=n,\\ k+l=m}} \begin{cases} \mathrm{NP}^{max}(h-1, \bar{i}, k) \\ \quad +\mathrm{VP}^{max}(\leq h-1, j, \bar{l}) \\ \mathrm{NP}^{max}(\leq h-1, \bar{i}, k) \\ \quad +\mathrm{VP}^{max}(h-1, j, \bar{l}) \end{cases}$$
$$\mathrm{NP}^{max}(h, \bar{n}, \bar{m}) = \max \begin{cases} \mathrm{NP}_1^{max}(h, \bar{n}, \bar{m}) \\ \mathrm{NP}_2^{max}(h, n, m) \end{cases}$$
$$\mathrm{NP}_1^{max}(h, \bar{n}, \bar{m}) = \max \begin{cases} \mathrm{N'}^{max}(h-1) \\ \quad +\mathrm{S}^{max}(\leq h-1, \overline{n-1}, \overline{m-1}) \\ \mathrm{N'}^{max}(\leq h-1) \\ \quad +\mathrm{S}^{max}(h-1, \overline{n-1}, \overline{m-1}) \end{cases}$$
$$\mathrm{NP}_1^{max}(h, n, \bar{m}) = \max \begin{cases} \mathrm{N'}^{max}(h-1) \\ \quad +\mathrm{S}^{max}(\leq h-1, n, \overline{m-1}) \\ \mathrm{N'}^{max}(\leq h-1) \\ \quad +\mathrm{S}^{max}(h-1, n, \overline{m-1}) \end{cases}$$
$$\mathrm{NP}_1^{max}(h, \bar{n}, m) = \max \begin{cases} \mathrm{N'}^{max}(h-1) \\ \quad +\mathrm{S}^{max}(\leq h-1, \overline{n-1}, m) \\ \mathrm{N'}^{max}(\leq h-1) \\ \quad +\mathrm{S}^{max}(h-1, \overline{n-1}, m) \end{cases}$$
$$\mathrm{NP}_2^{max}(h, n, m) = \begin{cases} \mathrm{N'}^{max}(h-1) & n = m = 0 \\ \text{undefined} & o.w. \end{cases}$$
$$\mathrm{VP}_1^{max}(h, n, \bar{m}) = \max \begin{cases} \mathrm{V}^{max}(h-1) \\ \quad +\mathrm{NP}^{max}(\leq h-1, n, \overline{m-1}) \\ \mathrm{V}^{max}(\leq h-1) \\ \quad +\mathrm{NP}^{max}(h-1, n, \overline{m-1}) \end{cases}$$

We think of functions in which overscores are written over some parameters as entirely different functions that have witnessed partial traversals through the cycles corresponding to the overscored parameters, beginning at the respective index nodes of those cycles.

Cycle variables are a local measure of non-terminal instances in that they do not depend on the absolute height of the tree — only on a fixed range of nodes above and below them in the tree. These makes them more suitable for the iterative computation of yields that we are interested in. Because X^{max} and X^{min} are now multivariate functions in general, we must tabulate an entire table out to some bound in each dimension, from which we obtain an entire frontier of acceptable values for the height and each cycle variable. Again, these can be posed either as interval constraints or finite domain constraints.

In the case of grammars over atomic categories, using a single cycle variable for every distinct cycle is generally not an option. The grammar induced from the local trees of the 35-sentence section wsj_0105 of the Penn Treebank II, for example, has 49 non-terminals and 258 rules, with 153,026 cycles. Grouping together cycles that differ only in their rule nodes, we are left with 204 groupings, and in fact, they pass through only 12 category nodes. Yet the category node with the largest number of incident cycles (NP) would still require 163 cycle (grouping) variables — too many to iteratively compute these functions efficiently. Naturally, it would be possible to conflate more cycles to obtain cruder but more efficient bounds.

References

G. E. Barton, R. C. Berwick, and E. S. Ristad. 1987. *Computational Complexity and Natural Language*. MIT Press.

M. Daniels and W. D. Meurers. 2002. Improving the efficiency of parsing with discontinuous constituents. In *7th International Workshop on Natural Language Understanding and Logic Programming (NLULP)*.

M. Johnson. 1985. Parsing with discontinuous constituents. In *Proceedings of the 23rd Annual Meeting of the Association for Computational Linguistics*, pages 127–132.

U. Moencke and R. Wilhelm. 1982. Iterative algorithms on grammar graphs. In H. J. Schneider and H. Goettler, editors, *Proceedings of the 8th Conference on Graphtheoretic Concepts in Computer Science (WG 82)*, pages 177–194. Carl Hanser Verlag.

F. Morawietz. 2000. Chart parsing and constraint programming. In *Proceedings of the 18th International Conference on Computational Linguistics (COLING-00)*, volume 1, pages 551–557.

G. Penn and M. Haji-Abdolhosseini. 2003. Topological parsing. In *Proceedings of the 10th Conference of the European Chapter of the Association for Computational Linguistics (EACL-03)*, pages 283–290.

F. C. N. Pereira and D. H. D. Warren. 1983. Parsing as deduction. In *Proceedings of 21st Annual Meeting of the Association for Computational Linguistics (ACL)*, pages 137–144.

M. Reape. 1991. Parsing bounded discontinuous constituents: Generalisations of some common algorithms. In M. Reape, editor, *Word Order in Germanic and Parsing*, pages 41–70. Centre for Cognitive Science, University of Edinburgh.

Numbat: Abolishing Privileges when Licensing New Constituents in Constraint-oriented Parsing

Jean-Philippe Prost
Centre for Language Technology
Macquarie University, Sydney, Australia
and *Laboratoire Parole et Langage*
Université de Provence, Aix-en-Provence, France
jpprost@ics.mq.edu.au

Abstract

The constraint-oriented approaches to language processing step back from the generative theory and make it possible, in theory, to deal with all types of linguistic relationships (e.g. dependency, linear precedence or immediate dominance) with the same importance when parsing an input utterance. Yet in practice, all implemented constraint-oriented parsing strategies still need to discriminate between "important" and "not-so-important" types of relations during the parsing process.

In this paper we introduce a new constraint-oriented parsing strategy based on *Property Grammars*, which overcomes this drawback and grants the same importance to all types of relations.

1 Introduction

In linguistics, the term *gradience* is often used to refer to the notion of acceptability as a gradient, as opposed to a more classical all-or-none notion. The research goal of this project is to build an experimental platform for computing gradience, i.e. for quantifying the degree of acceptability of an input utterance. We called this platform Numbat.

In order to be able to quantify such a gradient of acceptability with no *a priori* opinion on the influence played by different types of linguistic relationships, we want to adopt a framework where no one type of (syntactic) relation (e.g. dependency, immediate dominance, or linear precedence) is preferred over the other ones. Although a constraint-oriented (CO) paradigm such as *Property Grammars* (Blache, 2001) theoretically does not rely on any preferred relations, we observe that the parsing strategies implemented so far (Morawietz and Blache, 2002; Balfourier et al., 2002; Dahl and Blache, 2004; VanRullen, 2005) do not account for such a feature of the formalism. The strategy we have designed overcomes that problem and allows for constituents to be licensed by any type of relation. Not only does our approach maintain a close connection between implementation and underpinning theory, but it also allows for the decisions made with respect to gradience to be better informed. The purpose of the present paper is to present this new parsing strategy, and to emphasise how it "abolishes the privilege" usually only granted to a subset of syntactic relationships.

Section 2 presents some background information about the CO approaches and briefly introduces the Property Grammars formalism. Section 3 exposes and discusses the parsing strategy implemented in Numbat. Section 4 then draws the conclusion.

2 Constraint-oriented Approaches

The main feature common to all Constraint-oriented approaches is that parsing is modelled as a Constraint Satisfaction Problem (CSP). Maruyama's Constraint Dependency Grammar (CDG) (Maruyama, 1990) is the first formalism to introduce the parsing process as a CSP solver. Several extensions of CDG have then been proposed (Heinecke et al., 1998; Duchier, 1999; Foth et al., 2004).

Menzel and colleagues (Heinecke et al., 1998; Foth et al., 2004) developed a weighted (or "graded") version of CDG. Their parsing strategies are explored in the context of robust parsing. These strategies are based on an over-generation of candidate solutions. In this approach the CSP is turned into an optimisation problem, where sub-optimal solutions are filtered out according to a function of the weights associated to the violated constraints, and the notion of well-formedness is replaced by one of optimality. Indeed, the over-generation introduces inconsistencies in the constraint system, which prevents the use of the con-

Proceedings of the 3rd Workshop on Constraints and Language Processing (CSLP-06), pages 17–24,
Sydney, July 2006. ©2006 Association for Computational Linguistics

straint system as a set of well-formedness conditions, since even a well-formed utterance violates a subset of constraints. Consequently it is not possible to distinguish an optimal structure of an ill-formed utterance from an optimal structure of a well-formed utterance.

Duchier (1999) relies on *set constraints* and *selection constraints*[1] to axiomatise syntactic well-formedness and provides a concurrent constraint programming account of the parsing process. With the *eXtended Dependency Grammar* (XDG) (Debusmann et al., 2004) the notion of dependency tree is further extended to "multi-dimensional" dependency graph, where each dimension (e.g. *Immediate Dominance* and *Linear Precedence*) is associated with its own set of well-formedness conditions (called *principles*). Duchier (2000) sees dependency parsing as a *configuration problem*, where given a finite set of components (nodes in a graph) and a set of constraints specifying how these components may be connected, the task consists of finding a solution tree.

It seems, to the best of our knowledge, that neither of these works around XDG attempts to account for ill-formedness.

The Property Grammars (PG), introduced by Blache (Blache, 2001; Blache, 2005)[2], step back from Dependency Grammar. Solving the constraint system no longer results in a dependency structure but in a phrase structure, whose granularity may be tailored from a shallow one (i.e. a collection of disconnected components) to a deep one (i.e. a single hierarchical structure of constituents) according to application requirements[3]. This feature makes the formalism well suited for accounting for both ill-formedness and well-formedness, which is a key requirement for our experimental platform.

Introducing degrees of acceptability for an utterance does not mean indeed that it should be done at the expense of well-formedness: we want our model to account for ill-formedness and yet to also be able to recognise and acknowledge when an utterance is well-formed. This requirement rules out Optimality-theoretic frameworks as well as the ones based on Maruyama's CDG. Note that this is not to say that the task could not be achieved in a CDG-based framework; simply at this stage there is no work based on CDG, which would combine both an account of well-formedness and of optimality. A CO framework based on PG seems therefore best-suited for our purpose. Meanwhile, though different parsing strategies have been proposed for PG (Morawietz and Blache, 2002; Balfourier et al., 2002; Dahl and Blache, 2004; VanRullen, 2005), none of these strategies implements the possibility afforded by the theory to rely on *any* type of constraint in order to license a (possibly ill-formed) constituent.

We will see in this paper how the parsing strategy implemented in Numbat overcomes this problem.

2.1 The *Property Grammars* Formalism

2.1.1 Terminology

Construction. In PG a *construction* can be a lexical item's Part-of-Speech, a phrase, or top-level constructions such as, for example, the Caused-motion or the Subject-auxiliary Inversion constructions. The notion of construction is similar to the one in Construction Grammar (CxG)[4], as in (Goldberg, 1995), where:

> Cx is a construction *iff* Cx is a form-meaning pair $\langle F_i, S_i \rangle$ such that some aspect of F_i or some aspect of S_i is not strictly predictable from Cx's component parts or from other previously established constructions.

In this paper we only focus on syntax. For us, at the syntactic level, a construction is defined by a *form*, where a form is specified as a list of properties. When building a traditional phrase structure (i.e. a hierarchical structure of *constituents*) a construction can be simply seen as a non-terminal.

Property. A *property* is a constraint, which models a relationship among constructions. PG pre-defines several types of properties, which are specified according to their semantics. Moreover, the framework allows for new types to be defined.

[1] Although they are referred to with the same name by their respective authors, Duchier's notion of *selection constraint* is not to be confused with Dahl's *selection constraints* (Dahl and Blache, 2004). The two notions are significantly different.

[2] The Property Grammars were defined on the basis of the 5P formalism (Bès and Blache, 1999).

[3] For a discussion regarding PG and parsing with variable granularity see (VanRullen, 2005).

[4] Blache (2004) discussed how PG can be used as a formal framework for CxG.

In Numbat, a property type is also called a *relation*. Section 2.1.2 briefly presents some of the pre-defined property types and their semantics.

Assignment. In PG an *assignment* is a list of constituents. Let's consider, for example, the three constituents DET, ADJ and N, the following lists are possible assignments: [DET], [ADJ], [DET, ADJ], [ADJ, N], [DET, N], [DET, ADJ, N], etc..

2.1.2 Some Pre-defined Property Types

Here are some property types pre-defined in PG. See (Blache, 2005) for more types and more detailed definitions.

Notation. We note:

- $\mathcal{K}$ a set of constructions, with $\{\mathcal{C}, \mathcal{C}_1, \mathcal{C}_2\} \in \mathcal{K}$;
- $\mathbb{C}$ a set of constituents, with $\{c, c_1, c_2\} \in \mathbb{C}$;
- $\mathcal{A}$ an assignment;
- ind a function such that $ind(c, \mathcal{A})$ is the index of c in $\mathcal{A}$;
- cx a function such that $cx(c)$ is the construction of c;
- $\mathcal{P}(\mathcal{C}_1,\ \mathcal{C}_2)[c_1, c_2, \mathcal{A}]$ or $(\mathcal{C}_1\ \mathcal{P}\ \mathcal{C}_2)[c_1, c_2, \mathcal{A}]$ the constraint such that the relation $\mathcal{P}$ parametered with $(\mathcal{C}_1, \mathcal{C}_2)$, applies to $[c_1, c_2, \mathcal{A}]$.

Linear Precedence ($\prec$).
By definition, $(\mathcal{C}_1\ \prec\ \mathcal{C}_2)[c_1, c_2, \mathcal{A}]$ holds iff

$$\begin{cases} cx(c_1) = \mathcal{C}_1, & \text{and} \\ cx(c_2) = \mathcal{C}_2, & \text{and} \\ \{c_1, c_2\} \in \mathcal{A}, & \text{and} \\ ind(c_1, \mathcal{A}) < ind(c_2, \mathcal{A}) & \end{cases}$$

Exclusion ($\not\Leftrightarrow$).
By definition, $(\mathcal{C}_1\ \not\Leftrightarrow\ \mathcal{C}_2)[c_1, c_2, \mathcal{A}]$ holds iff

$$\begin{cases} cx(c_1) = \mathcal{C}_1, & \text{and} \\ cx(c_2) = \mathcal{C}_2, & \text{and} \\ \{c_1, c_2\} \cap \mathcal{A} \neq \{c_1, c_2\} & \end{cases}$$

Uniqueness ($Uniq$).
By definition, $Uniq(\mathcal{C})[c, \mathcal{A}]$ holds iff

$$\begin{cases} cx(c) = \mathcal{C}, & \text{and} \\ c \in \mathcal{A}, & \text{and} \\ \forall c' \in \mathcal{A} \backslash \{c\}, cx(c') \neq \mathcal{C} & \end{cases}$$

2.2 Related Problems

CO parsing with PG is an intersection of different classes of constraint-related problems, each of which is listed below.

Configuration problem. Given a set of components and a set of constraints specifying how these components can be connected, a configuration problem consists of finding a solution tree which connects the components together. Deep parsing with PG is a configuration problem where the components are constituents, and the resulting structure is a phrase structure. By extension, a solution to such a problem is called a *configuration*. A configuration problem can be modelled with a (static) CSP.

Dynamic CSP. In our case the problem is actually dynamic, in that the set of constraints to be solved evolves by the addition of new constraints. As we will see it later new constituents are inferred during the parsing process, and subsequently new constraints are dynamically added to the system. When dealing with deep parsing, i.e. with well-formedness only, the problem can be tackled as a *Dynamic CSP*, and solving techniques such as *Local Search* (Verfaillie and Schiex, 1994) can be applied.

Optimisation problem. In order to account for ill-formedness as well as well-formedness, we need to allow constraint relaxation, which turns the problem into an optimisation one. The expected outcome is thus an optimal configuration with respect to some valuation function. Should the input be well-formed, no constraints are relaxed and the expected outcome is a full parse. Should the input be ill-formed, constraints are relaxed and the expected outcome is either an optimal full parse or a set of (optimal) partial parses.

3 Numbat Architecture

3.1 The Parsing Strategy in Numbat

Relying on a design pattern used in various optimisation techniques, such as *dynamic programming*, the top-level strategy adopted in Numbat consists in three main steps:

1. splitting the problem into overlapping sub-problems;
2. solving the sub-problems—or building optimal sub-solutions;

3. building an optimal global solution, using the sub-solutions.

More specifically, the strategy adopted proceeds by successive *generate-and-test*: the possible models to local systems are generated, then their satisfiability is tested against the grammar. The partial solutions are re-injected in the process dynamically, and the basic process is iterated again. Note that the generate-and-test method is not compulsory and is only chosen here because it allows us to conveniently control and then filter the assignments.

Given an input utterance, the parsing process is made up of a re-iteration of the basic following steps:

1. **Building Site**. Build a set of constituents;

2. **Assignation**. Build all the possible assignments, i.e. all the possible combinations of one or more constituents;

3. **Checkpoint Alpha**. Filter out illegal assignments;

4. **Appropriation**. For every assignment, identify and build all the relevant properties among its elements, which leaves us with a property store, i.e. a constraint system;

5. **Checkpoint Bravo**. Filter out illegal assignments and irrelevant properties;

6. **Satisfaction**. Solve the constraint system;

7. **Formation**. Identify forms of construction, i.e. subsets of properties from the property store and nominate the corresponding candidate constructions;

8. **Polling booth**. Decide which of the candidate constructions are licensed and carried over to the next iteration;

The process stops when no new constituent can be built.

Each of these steps is defined in the following section.

3.1.1 Building Site

During the first iteration, this phase builds one constituent for each Part-of-Speech (POS) associated with an input word. From the second iteration onwards, new constituents are built provided the candidate assignments output by the previous round.

3.1.2 Assignation

From one iteration to the next new assignments are built, involving at least one of the new constituents. These constituents result from the previous iteration. Notice that the amount of new assignments created by each iteration grows exponentially with the amount of constituents (the 'old' ones and the new ones). Fortunately, the next step will filter out a large proportion of them.

This phase of assignation is essential to the process, and makes Numbat different from any other parsing strategy for PG. The difference will be made clear in the Satisfaction phase.

3.1.3 Checkpoint Alpha

In Numbat we use a *filtering profile* to specify which combination of heuristics applies during the parsing process. This feature proves to be very useful when performing experiments, as it allows an incremental approach, in order to determine the relative importance of each of the criteria on gradience by turning on and off one or other heuristic.

The heuristics play different roles. They are primarily used to prune the search space as early as possible in the process. Meanwhile, most of them capture language specific aspects (e.g. Contiguity, see below). These language specific heuristics are already present in previous works on PG in one form or another. We are working in the same framework and accept these restrictions, which might be relaxed by future work on the formal side.

During Checkpoint Alpha the following heuristics may apply.

Heuristic 1 (Distinct Constituents) *An assignment may contain no pairwise intersecting constituents.*

That is, any two constituents may not have any constituent in common. For example, the constituents {DET1, ADJ2} and {ADJ2, NOUN3} may not belong to the same assignment, since they have one constituent in common.

Heuristic 2 (Contiguity) *An assignment is a set of contiguous elements.*

This heuristic rules out crossing-over elements. Although this heuristic has little consequence when dealing with languages such as French or English, it may have to be turned off for languages with cross-serial dependencies such as Dutch. But if turned off, an additional problem then occurs that the semantics of pre-defined property types must be re-defined. The linear precedence, for instance, would need to account for the order between two crossing-over phrases, which is not the case in the current definition. On the other hand, notice that long distance dependencies are *not* ruled out by heuristic 2, since nested constituents are still legal.

3.1.4 Appropriation

This step has to do with the gathering of all the properties relevant to every assignment from the grammar. This operation is made easier by preprocessing the grammar, which is done at an initialisation step. During this preliminary phase, a lookup table is created for the grammar, where all the properties are indexed by their operands. Every property is also linked directly to the constructions for which it participates in the definition—i.e. the constructions for which the property is a member of the form. This table is actually a hash table, where the keys are the constructions on which the properties hold. For example, the property (Det $\prec$ Noun) is indexed by the couple of constructions (Det, Noun). And the property ($\{$Pronoun, Adv$\}$ $\not\Leftrightarrow$ V) is indexed by the triplets of constructions (Pronoun, Adv, V). Thus, given an assignment, i.e. a set of constituents, all we have to do here is to retrieve all the relevant properties from the lookup table, using all the (relevant) combinations of constituents as keys.

3.1.5 Checkpoint Bravo

Filters apply here, which aim to prune again the search space. The following heuristics may apply.

Heuristic 3 (Full Coverage) *Every element of an assignment must be involved in at least one constraint. That is, for each element in an assignment there must be at least one constraint defined over this element.*

Example 1 *Consider the assignment* $\mathcal{A} = \langle Det, N, V \rangle$*, and the grammar made up of the following properties:*

$$\text{VP} ::= \{V \prec \text{NP}\} \quad (1)$$
$$\text{NP} ::= \{Uniq(\text{N}),\ Det \prec \text{N},\ \text{N} \prec Adj\} \quad (2)$$
$$\text{S} ::= \{\text{NP} \prec \text{VP}\} \quad (3)$$

According to heuristic 3 $\mathcal{A}$ *is ruled out, since the V element is not* covered *by any constraints, whether we build an NP or a VP.*

Notice that this heuristic is semantically equivalent to the *Constituency* property present in early versions of PG[5]. The *Constituency* property used to specify which types of constituent (i.e. constructions) were legal ones (for a construction). Such a constraint is unnecessary since the information can be retrieved by simply listing all the types of constituents used in the definitions of properties. In example 1 for instance, the set of legal constituents for the NP construction is $[Det, N, Adj]$.

A main reason for dealing with constituency as a filter rather than as a constraint is to improve efficiency by reducing the amount of constraints in the system. Indeed, a filter aims to rule out constraints, which are subsequently removed from the constraint system. If dealt with as a constraint itself, Constituency would only make the constraint system more complex.

Heuristic 3 raises the issue of ruling out assignments with "free" constituents, i.e. constituents which are not connected to the rest of the assignment. Such a situation may occur, for example, in the case of an unknown word, either because it is absent from the lexicon, or misspelled. We choose to leave it up to the grammar writer to design their own *ad hoc* solutions regarding how to handle such cases. It may be done, for instance, through the definition of a "wildcard construction", and perhaps also a "wildcard property type", which will be used appropriately in the grammar.

3.1.6 Satisfaction

At this stage, only legal assignments and relevant properties are kept in the system. All the required information for evaluating the properties is thus available and all we have to do now is to solve the constraint system.

The solver we use is implemented in Constraint Handling Rules (CHR) (Frühwirth, 1994). Unlike other CHR implementations of PG (Morawietz and Blache, 2002; Dahl and Blache, 2004) where the semantics of the property types are encoded in the handlers[6]—and therefore each type of property requires a different handler—, the approach we have adopted allows us to externalise the semantics and to generalise the properties evaluation with one single handler. The algorithm un-

[5]The *Constituency* property is discarded in the version of PG underpinning Numbat.

[6]A CHR handler is a rule of the general form `(A => B | C)`, which can be read "if A then (if B then C)"

derlying this handler can be expressed as follows:

for each (list of n *constituents, assignment, property*)

if (the list of n *constituents* and the *assignment* match the *property*'s ones)

then

if (*property* is satisfied)

then (tick *property* as being SATISFIED)

else (tick *property* as being VIOLATED)

The CHR handler takes the following form:

```
listOfConstituents(Ccs) &&
assignment(Asg) &&
property(Pp) ==>
  Pp.isConsistentWith(Asg,Ccs) |
    (Pp.isSatisfied() ->
      sat(Pp) ; unSat(Pp)).
```

3.1.7 Formation

This phase is concerned with identifying the constructions in the grammar which can be triggered (i.e. licensed) by the properties present in the property store. A construction is *triggered* by any of the properties which are used to define this construction. This task can be performed easily by accessing them directly in the lookup table (see section 3.1.4), using a property's operands as the key. The constructions which are triggered are called *target constructions*. We then build a constituent for each of these target construction. Such a constituent is called a *candidate constituent*.

This phase basically builds constituent structures. During the next iteration these candidates may be used in turn as constituents. The process thus accounts for recursive structures as well as non-recursive ones. Meanwhile, it is interesting to emphasise that building such a constituent structure is not necessary when parsing with PG. We could, for instance, deal with the whole sentence at once as a sequence of word order constraints. This way no constituent structure would be needed to license infinite sets of strings. In this case, the efficiency of such a process is something that has been worked on extensively within the CSP field. What we are contributing is merely a representation and translation to CSP, which allows us to take advantage of these efficiencies that decades of other work have produced.

Monotonic and Non-monotonic Constraints. The notions of *Selection Constraint* in (Dahl and Blache, 2004) and of *non-Lacunar Constraint* in (VanRullen, 2005) are equivalent and denote a class of constraint types, whose semantics is monotonic, in that their satisfiability does not change when new elements are added to the assignment. Constraint types such as Linear Precedence or Obligation, for example, are monotonic. On the other hand the constraint $Uniq(\mathcal{C})[c, \mathcal{A}]$ (see 2.1.2), for example, is non-monotonic: if the contextual assignment $\mathcal{A}$ grows—i.e. if new constituents are added to it—the constraint needs to be re-evaluated. In parsing strategies where the assignments are built dynamically by successive additions of new constituents, the evaluation of the relevant constraints is performed on the fly, which means that the non-monotonic constraints need to be re-evaluated every time the assignment grows. This problem is tackled in different ways, according to implementation. But we observe that in all cases, the decision to trigger new candidate constituents relies only on the evaluation of the monotonic constraints. The decision process usually simply ignores the non-monotonic ones. Numbat, by fixing the assignments prior to evaluating the local constraint systems, includes both the monotonic and the non-monotonic constraints in the licensing process (i.e. in the Formation phase).

3.1.8 Polling Booth

This phase is concerned with the election process, which leads to choosing the candidates who will make it to the next iteration.

The following heuristics may apply.

Heuristic 4 (Minimum Satisfaction) *An assignment is valid only if at least one constraint holds on any of its constituents.*

Notice that in all other implementations of PG this heuristic is much more restrictive and requires that a *monotonic* constraint must hold.

Heuristic 5 (Full Input Span) *A valid (partial or final) solution to the parsing problem is either a single constituent which spans exactly the input utterance, or a combination of constituents (i.e. a combination of partial parses) which spans exactly the input utterance.*

In theory, we want the Polling Booth to build all the candidate constituents we have identified, and re-inject them in the system for new iterations. In practice, different strategies may apply in order to prune the search space, such as strategies based on the use of a ranking function. In our case, every iteration of the parsing process only propagates one valid combination of constituents to the next iteration (e.g. the best one according to a valuation function). Somehow such a strategy corresponds to always providing the main process with a "disambiguated" set of input constituents from one iteration to another. This heuristic may also be used as a termination rule.

A question then arises regarding the relaxation policy: Do all the constraint types carry same importance with respect to relaxation? This question addresses the relative importance of different constraint types with respect to acceptability. Does, for instance, the violation of a constraint of Linear Precedence between a Determiner and a Noun in a Noun Phrase have the same impact on the overall acceptability of the Noun Phrase than the violation of Uniqueness of the Noun (still within a Noun Phrase)? From a linguistic point of view, the answer to that question is not straightforward and requires number of empirical studies. Some works have been carried out (Gibson, 2000; Keller, 2000), which aim to provide elements of answer in very targeted syntactic contexts.

The impact that the relaxation of different constraint types has on acceptability should not be biased by a particular parsing strategy. Thus, the framework provides the linguist (and the grammar writer) with maximum flexibility when it comes to decide the cost of relaxing different types of constraint on acceptability, since *any type* may be relaxed. Intuitively, one can clearly relax (in French) a constraint of Agreement in gender between determiner and noun; on the other hand one could not as easily relax constraints of type Obligation, which are often used to specify heads. A complete breakdown of constraints into relaxable and non-relaxable is future work. But at the end, the parser just produces sets of satisfied and violated constraints, regardless of how important they are. There will then be a separate process for predicting gradience, where the relative importance of particular constraints in determining acceptability will be decided experimentally.

4 Conclusion

In this paper we have presented the constraint-oriented parsing strategy based on Property Grammars, that we have developed as part of the Numbat platform. We have also demonstrated that, unlike other existing parsers for PG, this strategy does not privilege any particular type of property when licensing a new constituent. By doing so, this parser contributes to maintain a close connection with the underpinning theory. In the context of robust parsing, where decisions must be made on the basis of a balance between satisfied and violated properties, it also allows the decision process to be better informed by providing it with more grounding linguistic material concerning the input.

For the same reason, this contribution is also fairly valuable in the context of our prime research goal, which is concerned with quantifying acceptability.

In further works we plan to evaluate the performance of the parser. We also plan to use Numbat to run series of experiments on gradience, in order to design and test a suitable valuation function to be used to assess the degree of acceptability of an input utterance.

References

Jean-Marie Balfourier, Philippe Blache, and Tristan Van Rullen. 2002. From Shallow to Deep Parsing Using Constraint Satisfaction. In *Proc. of the 6th Int'l Conference on Computational Linguistics (COLING 2002)*.

Gabriel Bès and Philippe Blache. 1999. Propriétés et analyse d'un langage. In *TALN*.

Philippe Blache. 2001. *Les Grammaires de Propriétés : des contraintes pour le traitement automatique des langues naturelles*. Hermès Sciences.

Philippe Blache. 2004. Constraints: an operational framework for constructions grammars. In *ICCG-04*, pages 25–26.

Philippe Blache. 2005. Property Grammars: A fully constraint-based theory. In Henning Christiansen, Peter Rossen Skadhauge, and Jorgen Villadsen, editors, *Constraint Solving and Language Processing*, volume 3438 of *LNAI*. Springer.

Veronica Dahl and Philippe Blache. 2004. Directly executable constraint based grammars. In *Journees Francophones de Programmation en Logique avec Contraintes*, pages 149–166, Angers, France.

Ralph Debusmann, Denys Duchier, and Geert-Jan M. Kruijff. 2004. Extensible Dependency Grammar: A New Methodology. In *Proceedings of the 7th International Conference on Computational Linguistics (COLING 2004)*.

Denys Duchier. 1999. Axiomatizing Dependency Parsing Using Set Constraints. In *Proceedings 6th Meeting on the Mathematics of Language*, Orlando, FL.

Denys Duchier. 2000. Configuration Of Labeled Trees Under Lexicalized Constraints And Principles. To appear in the Journal of Language and Computation, December.

Kilian Foth, Wolfgang Menzel, and Ingo Schrder. 2004. Robust Parsing with Weighted Constraints. *Natural Language Engineerings*.

Thom Frühwirth. 1994. Theory and Practice of Constraint Handling Rules. *The Journal of Logic Programming*, 37((1-3)), October. Special Issue on Constraint Logic Programming.

Edward Gibson. 2000. The Dependency Locality Theory: A Distance-Based Theory of Linguistic Complexity. In Alec Marantz, Yasushi Miyashita, and Wayne ONeil, editors, *Image, Language, Brain*, pages 95–126. Cambridge, Mass., MIT Press.

Adele Goldberg. 1995. *Constructions: A Construction Grammar Approach to Argument Structure*. Chicago University Press.

Johannes Heinecke, Jürgen Kunze, Wolfgang Menzel, and Ingo Shröder. 1998. Eliminative Parsing with Graded Constraints. In *Proc. 7th CoLing conf., 36th Annual Meeting of the ACL*, volume Coling–ACL '98, pages pp. 526–530, Montreal, Canada.

Frank Keller. 2000. *Gradience in Grammar - Experimental and Computational Aspects of Degrees of Grammaticality*. Ph.D. thesis, University of Edinburgh.

Hiroshi Maruyama. 1990. Structural Disambiguation with Constraint Propagation. In *Proceedings 28th Annual Meeting of the ACL*, pages pp. 31–38, Pittburgh, PA.

Frank Morawietz and Philippe Blache. 2002. Parsing natural languages with chr. Under consideration for publication in Theory and Practice of Logic Programming.

Tristan VanRullen. 2005. *Vers une analyse syntaxique à granularité variable*. Ph.D. thesis, Université de Provence, Informatique.

Gérard Verfaillie and Thomas Schiex. 1994. Solution reuse in dynamic CSPs. In *AAAI '94: Proc. of the twelfth national conf. on AI (vol. 1)*, pages 307–312, Menlo Park, CA, USA. American Ass. for AI.

Pragmatic Constraints on Semantic Presupposition

Yafa Al-Raheb
National Centre for Language Technology
School of Computing
Dublin City University, Ireland
yafa.alraheb@gmail.com

Abstract

The literature investigating the notion of presupposition in Discourse Representation Theory (DRT) has mainly been dubbed as being semantic (Simons 2003). This paper investigates the linguistic application of pragmatic-based constraints to the 'semantic' notion of presupposition in DRT. By applying pragmatic-based constraints to presuppositional phenomenon, we aim to defend DRT against the accusation that DRT's interpretation of presuppositional phenomenon is essentially 'semantic' and push this interpretation further towards the pragmatic side of the semantic/pragmatic interface.[1]

1 Introduction

Devising an appropriate theory of presupposition has been one of the main issues in semantics, pragmatics and most recently computational linguistics. Indeed, many theorists have argued extensively about the definition that captures the meaning of presupposition and whether presuppositions are a property of the utterance or of the speaker. Developments in dynamic semantics, as opposed to static semantics, resulting in DRT, have led to a framework suitable for the representation of linguistic phenomenon. Some of DRT's principal concerns are with finding the right truth conditions and interpretation for referential expressions, specifically anaphora. This is relevant for further investigation of 'pragmatic' presupposition because it has in fact been proposed by van der Sandt and Geurts (1991) that it is anaphora that lies at the basis of presupposition.

However, Simons (2003) has recently noted some pragmatic limitations in the present state of DRT. She refers in the following quotation to 'dynamic semantics', the field taken to include DRT.

> Dynamic semantics does not attempt to understand presupposition and presuppositional constraints in terms of the speaker's beliefs and intentions, or to root presuppositional constraints in terms of the broad goals of communicators (Simons 2003: 27).

Indeed, Simons concludes that DRT is a theory of semantic and not pragmatic presupposition (2003). The criticism that DRT is only semantic is not wholly justified. While DRT stems from the need for appropriate semantic representation of discourse, DRT does recognize the importance of context in representing referents in discourse, which is generally taken to mark a pragmatic perspective on presupposition. Additionally, theories within DRT, such as the Binding Theory (Geurts 1999), have attempted to make DRT more pragmatic; in particular, Presupposition as Anaphora Theory's construction process of presupposition (van der Sandt and Geurts 1991). However, while this paper aims to show that DRT is not entirely devoid of pragmatics, it argues that DRT is in need of a more pragmatic treatment of presupposition, which (a) pays more attention to the beliefs and intentions of the speaker and the hearer and their relation to presupposition and (b) makes presuppositional constraints more precise. Further, other scholars have criticized DRT for being essentially truthconditional. Werth, for example, claims that DRT is essentially only about truthconditionality:

[1] I gratefully acknowledge support from Science Foundation Ireland grant 04/IN/I527.

Proceedings of the 3rd Workshop on Constraints and Language Processing (CSLP-06), pages 25–32,
Sydney, July 2006. ©2006 Association for Computational Linguistics

> [DRT's] goal is truth-conditionality and its models are minimal worlds inhabited by predicates and variables... it does not model human understanding: there is no place in it for participant roles, setting, background knowledge, purposes, even inferences (Werth 1999: 65).

Again, this criticism is not entirely just. To address the aforementioned pragmatic limitations of DRT, the aim of this paper is to address the problem of insightfully capturing pragmatic constraints on presuppositional phenomenon within the framework of DRT. To achieve this, a pragmatically-constrained definition of presupposition is attempted. This is followed by setting some pragmatic constraints on agents' conception of presuppositional phrases based on the agents' roles in conversation. An example of how these pragmatic constraints operate in DRT is then examined. Furthermore, an overall structure computationally encompassing these pragmatic constraints in DRT is described.

2 Pragmatic-based Presupposition

In linguistics the treatment of presupposition has generally been split between two camps, semantics and pragmatics. Karttunen (1973) maintains that the semantic perspective on presupposition sees presupposition as emanating from the sentence, and the pragmatic perspective as emanating from the speaker. Levinson argues that presupposition cannot be viewed as semantic in the narrow sense (based on formal logic and truth conditionality), but rather as dependent on context and 'the actual linguistic structure of sentences' (Levinson 1983: 167). Theories defining presupposition within pragmatics depend mainly on mutual knowledge (or common ground).

Within computational linguistics the treatment of presupposition falls mainly within dynamic semantics, within which DRT has developed. In the broadest terms presupposition, whether in linguistics or philosophy, has been viewed as a relation between sentences or propositions, where the presupposed proposition is not in focus in the presupposition sentence. DRT, and dynamic semantics in general, is precisely concerned with such relations – i.e. with the relations between an utterance and previous utterances in the discourse.

Given these varying definitions as to what constitutes presupposition, before attempting to introduce pragmatic constraints to presupposition in DRT, we must first explain what pragmatic presupposition, as used in this paper, constitutes. Two important notions come into question when assessing what constitutes presupposition, namely, the notion of givenness and the relationship between the beliefs (or the cognitive states) of the agents involved in a conversation.

2.1 Presupposition and Givenness

While presuppositions can be defined as that part of the utterance that is taken to be 'given' (Lambrecht 1994), the notion of 'given' needs clarifying. 'Given' means known information, information that the speaker regards as known to both speaker and hearer - information directly relating to the topic of the dialogue or as part of general background knowledge assumptions about the world. The presupposition in this sense is a reflection of the speaker's assumptions about the hearer's state of mind, i.e. the speaker assumes the hearer already knows this information (Lambrecht 1994). An alternate meaning of 'given' is when the speaker knows that the information the presupposition provides is, in fact, new to the hearer. In this case, the speaker introduces the new information 'as if' it were given, in order to indicate that the presupposed information is not the focus of the speaker's attention. Unlike Stalnaker's understanding of presupposition (Stalnaker 2002), this understanding of 'given' to include information new to the hearer means that the presupposition introduced is not necessarily part of what is often termed the 'common ground'.

Thus, we might think in terms of a speaker 'packaging' information as a presupposition (speaker presupposition). In this approach, the speaker has the choice of picking information she deems to be known to the hearer or information that she deems to be new to the hearer, knowing that to do so, she (the speaker) is communicating that the presupposition is not the focus of her utterance, but rather she would like the hearer to direct his attention to the new information provided by the rest of the utterance. For new, presupposed information to pass as given, the speaker must be aware that introducing an 'out of the ordinary' or 'remarkable' presupposition will cause problems. For instance, example (1) is less likely to cause problems than example (2) when the hearer knows that the speaker lives in the city centre.

(1) The car across the street from my house belongs to my neighbour.

(2) The small jet across the street from my house belongs to my neighbour,

2.2 Presupposition and Agents' Cognitive States

To define pragmatic presupposition within DRT, presupposition should be understood to be a property of the agent. Lambrecht (1994) understands pragmatic presupposition as an interest in the assumptions speakers make about hearers. There are two types of agent presupposition, speaker presupposition and hearer presupposition. This is different from semantic presupposition, i.e. sentence presupposition. Agent presupposition differs from sentence presupposition in that the latter stems from sentence meaning, whereas the former attaches itself to the beliefs of the speaker and her intentions.

In essence, the effect of presupposition is to give insights about the speaker's beliefs as well as the speaker's beliefs about the hearer's beliefs. In this sense, the dynamic semantic notion of 'taken for granted' means that the speaker believes the presupposition to be either known information or information that is not the desired focus of attention. When a speaker introduces a presupposition in her utterance, she is not primarily concerned with the information the presupposition provides, but rather in the new information, the 'assertion' part, the utterance communicates.

Presupposition is related to the beliefs of the speaker. Speaker belief leads to presupposition, which indicates the beliefs of the speaker to the hearer. Presupposition is a reflection of the speaker's state of mind. What speakers presuppose gives an indication as to what speakers believe or accept (weakly believe) and what they believe hearers believe or accept within the context of a dialogue (cf. Al-Raheb 2005). This is stronger than what is generally conceded in the relevant literature (Geurts 1999).

While this view of pragmatic presupposition shares Stalnaker's (2002) view concerning the importance of beliefs and context to understanding linguistic phenomena, the present view of presupposition has a different understanding of the relationship between belief and presupposition. Stalnaker sees beliefs, not in terms of the speaker, but rather in terms of the vague term the 'common ground' (cf. Al-Raheb 2005). '[T]o believe p to be common ground is to presuppose in Stalnaker's sense' as Simons (2003: 19) puts it. The view presented here takes the position that presuppositions reflect the speaker's beliefs, regardless of whether the beliefs are part of common ground or not.

3 Pragmatic Constraints

Having defined what is meant by pragmatic presupposition, we now move to discuss introducing pragmatic constraints on the phenomenon of presupposition in DRT. In order to enhance the pragmatic representation of presuppositional phenomenon in DRT, Gricean maxims need to be formulated in terms of pragmatic constraints on generating presuppositional utterances (speaker's perspective) and interpreting them (hearer's perspective). The maxims are reformulated in terms of the cognitive relationship between the speaker and the hearer, producing constraints on presupposition which are necessary for successful communication.

Following Grice's Cooperative Principle (Grice 1989), by adhering to the maxims, dialogue agents are being cooperative and not attempting to deceive or lie to one another (Grice 1989). The intention to communicate requires the speaker to assess her beliefs concerning the hearer's beliefs. This way of thinking about dialogue communication leads to the formulation of pragmatic constraints. It is proposed that these constraints broadly correspond to Grice's quantity and quality maxims. Section 4 describes an implementation of the pragmatic constraints introduced in this section.

To make her contribution informative (maxim of quantity), the speaker needs to follow the first pragmatic constraint placed on making an assertion (BCA1): to express an assertion the speaker needs to believe that the hearer does not hold the assertion, A, as a belief. In other words, the speaker believes the hearer does not hold the belief that A. This is similar to van der Sandt's (1992) informativity constraint, although his informativity constraint is not directly linked to beliefs. This pragmatic constraint is illustrated in the following example:

(3) Speaker: Mia likes dancing.
Hearer: Yeah I know.

In example (3) the hearer indicates previous knowledge of A, which means that either the speaker is not following BCA1, or that the speaker was not aware that the hearer believes A. With each new utterance, the speaker must be aware of the BCA1.

The second pragmatic constraint placed on assertion is BCA2. Following from our assumptions concerning Grice's quality maxim, for a speaker to express an assertion, the speaker must herself believe or accept that assertion. That is to say, being cooperative, to express A, the speaker must believe or accept that A.

Similarly, to introduce a presupposition, the speaker must include the presupposition in her beliefs or acceptance space (quality maxim), (BCP1). If the speaker is initiating a topic, the hearer has more grounds to conclude the speaker believes P (BCP1a). At the same time, the speaker must also be aware that when introducing P, the speaker is communicating that the speaker believes P. That is to say, if the speaker initiates the topic of P, the hearer may assume that the speaker believes P. However, when it is the hearer's turn to become the speaker, and he refers to the presupposition, P, introduced by the speaker, the speaker, who introduced P, may assume a weaker belief on the part of the hearer, namely that the hearer accepts P. Thus, presuppositions are built on the current context, which is built upon the union of beliefs and acceptance spaces of an agent. In other words, if the hearer refers to a presupposition employed previously by the speaker, the hearer (who now becomes the speaker) at least accepts P (i.e. holds P in his acceptance space) (BCP2).

For example,

(4) S1: I must buy Vincent's wife a birthday present.
H1: I didn't know Vincent was married.
S2: Yes, he is. His wife likes chocolate.
H2: She may also like flowers.
S3: I'll buy her chocolates.

The speaker initiates the presupposition (in example (4) it is new information to the hearer) that Vincent has a wife. According to BCP1, the hearer may safely assume and indeed add to his beliefs about the speaker's beliefs that the speaker believes P (Vincent has a wife). However, when the hearer comes to refer to P (Vincent's wife), the speaker does not necessarily infer that the hearer believes Vincent is married, but rather that the hearer accepts P. Introducing a topic for the presupposition allows the hearer to add more strength to her representation of the speaker's beliefs, i.e. to establish belief rather than acceptance. This would be more evident in a context where the speaker is attempting to persuade the hearer to do something. For information dialogues, where the information provider has the authority of possessing the answers to the information seeker's questions, the beliefs of the information provider may attain a stronger position than they would in other types of social contexts (cf. Al-Raheb 2005). The information seeker is less likely to challenge or evaluate the strength of belief of the information provider. If we contrast example (4) with example (5), the strength of beliefs are much higher, we can assume, than for when the hearer is not required to perform any action.

(5) S1: You should buy Vincent's wife a birthday present.
H1: I didn't know Vincent was married.
S2: Yes he is. His wife likes chocolate.
H2: She may also like flowers.
S3: But she prefers chocolate.
H3: I'll get her some chocolate.

In example (4), where the hearer was not required to perform any action, it is safer for the speaker to assume that the hearer accepts P as the hearer is not committing himself to doing any task, than to assume the stronger case, i.e. the hearer believes P. However, in example (5) where the hearer agrees to buying Vincent's wife a present in H3 (that is the hearer commits to perform an action for Vincent's wife), the speaker will conclude that the hearer believes the presupposed proposition and adds this to the speaker's representation of the hearer's beliefs. In other words, when the hearer makes P, in H3, the speaker concludes that the hearer believes P and adds this to the speaker's representation, or beliefs set, of the hearer's beliefs. Thus, someone getting someone else's commitment to do something implies greater strength of belief about a presupposition which affects that commitment.

Allowing the hearer to assume weaker belief brings us back to Simons' (2003) suggestion of modifying Stalnaker's understanding of presupposition to become what she terms the 'disposition of presupposition': speakers 'act as if' they take the presupposition for granted. Simons (2003) argues that speakers do not need to believe the presuppositions they use. With acceptance, as understood by the view of pragmatic presupposition presented in this paper, speakers do not have to hold the strong belief P. But, at the same time, to express P, speakers should not hold the belief that P is false. That is, being cooperative necessitates that when the speaker utters P, the speaker does not hold the belief that $\neg$ P. Speakers may indicate stronger belief. However, if there is no such indication (e.g. 'Definitely', or 'I couldn't agree more'), hearers may conclude that speakers at least hold the presupposition in their acceptance space. Speakers may later allow the hearer to conclude that they hold greater strength of belief than at first assumed.

4 Implementing Pragmatic Constraints

The following set of operations implement the pragmatic constraints on presupposition and assertion set out in section 3, namely BCA1, BCA2, BCP1, and BCP2.[2] We begin, firstly, by showing how the pragmatic constraint operations are implemented and by demonstrating how the code works on linear DRSs (cf. Al-Raheb 2005). Secondly, we demonstrate how the constraints work on a real example by passing an example dialogue through the implemented pragmatic constraints for both the speaker and the hearer.

4.1 Implementation

The first pragmatic constraint on assertion (BCA1) is represented by beliefConstraintA1. It checks that a condition is not in the hearer's Belief DRS nor inside the hearer's Acceptance DRS in a Speaker's Belief or Acceptance DRS. Agent's Belief DRSs represent stronger beliefs they hold and stronger beliefs they have about other agents in dialogue, whereas Acceptance DRSs represent their weaker beliefs about the dialogue and about the weaker beliefs held by other agents in dialogue (cf. Al-Raheb 2005). When a condition is not found in either embedded DRS, it succeeds.

The second pragmatic constraint on assertion (BCA2) is represented by beliefConstraintA2, which checks if a condition is either in the speaker's Belief or Acceptance DRS. The operation succeeds once a match is found.[3] BCP1

```
drs1:drs([x, z],
    [walter(x),
    vincent(z),
    attitude(i, 'BEL', drs2),
    drs2:drs([ ],
        [attitude(you, 'BEL', drs3),
        drs3:drs([ ],
            [ ]) ]),
    attitude(i, 'ACCEPT', drs4),
    drs4:drs([ ],
        [c1: dancer(z),
        attitude(you, 'ACCEPT', drs5),
        drs5:drs([ ],
            [ ]) ]) ]).
```

becomes:

```
drs1:drs([x, z],
    [walter(x),
    vincent(z),
    attitude(i, 'BEL', drs2),
    drs2:drs([ ],
        [attitude(you, 'BEL', drs3),
        drs3:drs([ ],
            [b1: singer(x) ]) ]),
    attitude(i, 'ACCEPT', drs4),
    drs4:drs([ ],
        [c1: dancer(z),
        attitude(you, 'ACCEPT', drs5),
        drs5:drs([ ],
            [ ]) ]) ]).
```

Figure 1: Hearer BCP1

has been subdivided into speaker and hearer. The *speaker* side, beliefConstraintSpeakerP1 checks if a condition is a member of the speaker's belief or acceptance DRS.

For the *hearer*, beliefConstraintHearerP1 checks if a condition is not a member of the speaker's acceptance or belief DRS, then checks if the condition is not a member of the hearer's belief or acceptance DRS. If this check passes, the condition is added to the hearer's belief about the speaker's belief, i.e. speaker's belief DRS embedded inside the hearer's DRS. When using 'beliefConstraintHearerP1' to check for the condition 'singer(X)', we get the second DRS as a result in Figure 1.

The second version of the hearer's BCP1, beliefConstraintHearerP1a, checks if a condition is not a member of the speaker's belief or acceptance DRS, and is a member of the hearer's belief or acceptance DRS. Then, it adds the condition to the speaker's acceptance DRS, embedded inside the hearer's acceptance DRS. This is shown in Figure 2.

The second pragmatic constraint on Presuppo-

[2]The implementation outlined in this section demonstrates how pragmatic constraints on presupposition can be implemented, but does not describe the entire architecture of checking that these constraints are adhered to in processing an entire dialogue.

[3]These pragmatic constraints on assertion are not demonstrated as the focus of this paper is presupposition.

```
drs1:drs([x, z],
    [walter(x),
    vincent(z),
    attitude(i, 'BEL', drs2),
    drs2:drs([ ],
        [b1: singer(x),
        attitude(you, 'BEL', drs3),
        drs3:drs([ ],
            [ ]) ]),
    attitude(i, 'ACCEPT', drs4),
    drs4:drs([ ],
        [c1: dancer(z),
        attitude(you, 'ACCEPT', drs5),
        drs5:drs([ ],
            [ ]) ]) ]).
```

becomes:

```
drs1:drs([x, z],
    [walter(x),
    vincent(z),
    attitude(i, 'BEL', drs2),
    drs2:drs([ ],
        [b1: singer(x),
        attitude(you, 'BEL', drs3),
        drs3:drs([ ],
            [ ]) ]),
    attitude(i, 'ACCEPT', drs4),
    drs4:drs([ ],
        [c1: dancer(z),
        attitude(you, 'ACCEPT', drs5),
        drs5:drs([ ],
            [c2: singer(x) ]) ]) ]).
```

Figure 2: Hearer BCP1a

```
drs1:drs([x, z],
    [walter(x),
    vincent(z),
    attitude(i, 'BEL', drs2),
    drs2:drs([ ],
        [b1: singer(x),
        attitude(you, 'BEL', drs3),
        drs3:drs([ ],
            [ ]) ]),
    attitude(i, 'ACCEPT', drs4),
    drs4:drs([ ],
        [c1: dancer(z),
        attitude(you, 'ACCEPT', drs5),
        drs5:drs([ ],
            [ ]) ]) ]).
```

becomes:

```
drs1:drs([x, z],
    [walter(x),
    vincent(z),
    attitude(i, 'BEL', drs2),
    drs2:drs([ ],
        [b1: singer(x),
        attitude(you, 'BEL', drs3),
        drs3:drs([ ],
            [ ]) ]),
    attitude(i, 'ACCEPT', drs4),
    drs4:drs([ ],
        [c1: dancer(z),
        attitude(you, 'ACCEPT', drs5),
        drs5:drs([ ],
            [c2: singer(x) ]) ]) ]).
```

Figure 3: Speaker BCP2

sition (BCP2) is also divided into speaker side and hearer side. The speaker's side, beliefConstraintSpeakerP2, checks a condition, e.g. 'singer(X)', is a member of the speaker's belief or acceptance DRS, but not a member of the hearer's acceptance or belief DRS, embedded inside the speaker's DRSs (Figure 3). Once this is fulfilled, the condition is added to the hearer's acceptance DRS, embedded inside the speaker's acceptance DRS.

BCP2, from the hearer's perspective, uses beliefConstraintHearerP2, which checks whether a condition, e.g. 'singer(X)', is a member of the speaker's belief or acceptance DRS (embedded inside the hearer's DRSs), and then checks if the condition is not a member of the hearer's acceptance or belief DRSs. It then adds the condition to the hearer's acceptance DRS, as in Figure 4.

4.2 Application

The following example

(6) S1: You have to buy Vincent's wife a present.
H1: Should I send Mia flowers?
S1: Mia likes chocolate. Buy her some.
H2: I'll buy her chocolate.

is passed through the implemented pragmatic constraints to briefly demonstrate how the pragmatic constraints can be employed in dialogue. Figures 5 and 6 show the initial beliefs of both agents before the dialogue is initiated. To proceed, the pragmatic constraints for the speaker are applied. If the pragmatic constraints do not apply, the dialogue cannot go forward. This starts a recognition process on the part of the hearer.

To utter S1, the speaker is constrained by BCP1 for the speaker, which dictates that the presupposition to be uttered needs to be part of the speaker's beliefs or acceptance DRSs (cf. section 3). When this is verified, the speaker is able to make an utterance containing the presupposition resulting

```
drs1:drs([x, z],
    [walter(x),
    vincent(z),
    attitude(i, 'BEL', drs2),
    drs2:drs([ ],
        [attitude(you, 'BEL', drs3),
        drs3:drs([ ],
            [b1: singer(x) ]) ]),
    attitude(i, 'ACCEPT', drs4),
    drs4:drs([ ],
        [c1: dancer(z),
        attitude(you, 'ACCEPT', drs5),
        drs5:drs([ ],
            [ ]) ]) ]).
```

becomes:

```
drs1:drs([x, z],
    [walter(x),
    vincent(z),
    attitude(i, 'BEL', drs2),
    drs2:drs([ ],
        [attitude(you, 'BEL', drs3),
        drs3:drs([ ],
            [b1: singer(x) ]) ]),
    attitude(i, 'ACCEPT', drs4),
    drs4:drs([ ],
        [c1: dancer(z),
        c2: singer(x),
        attitude(you, 'ACCEPT', drs5),
        drs5:drs([ ],
            [ ]) ]) ]).
```

Figure 4: Hearer BCP2

in Figure 7.[4] Here, the speaker already believes the hearer believes the contents of the presupposition, 'Vincent has a wife', and as such nothing needs to be changed in the speaker's beliefs about the hearer's beliefs, BCP2 for the speaker. If, however, the speaker did not already believe the hearer believes the presupposition, the contents of the presupposition would be added to the hearer's acceptance DRS inside the speaker's acceptance DRS according to BCP2 for the speaker.

In the process of recognizing the speaker's utterance, the hearer's pragmatic constraints are employed and if they are violated, again the dialogue cannot proceed. The first pragmatic constraint for the hearer to apply is BCP1, which checks whether both the speaker and the hearer do not believe or accept the presupposition. Upon finding that both the speaker and the hearer believe the presupposition, there is no need to add anything to either the hearer's or the speaker's belief and acceptance spaces. If, however, that was not the case, BCP1 and BCP1a alter the hearer's and speaker's belief states accordingly by adding the contents of the presupposition as indicated in section 4.1. The same reasoning applies to checking whether BCP2 applies, for if the hearer did not already believe or accept the presupposition, BCP2 adds the contents of the presupposition to the hearer's acceptance DRS. After this, the speaker's pragmatic constraints are checked against the hearer's, who is now the speaker, utterance and so on.

[4]Figures 7 and 8 show both agents' beliefs after S1 is uttered.

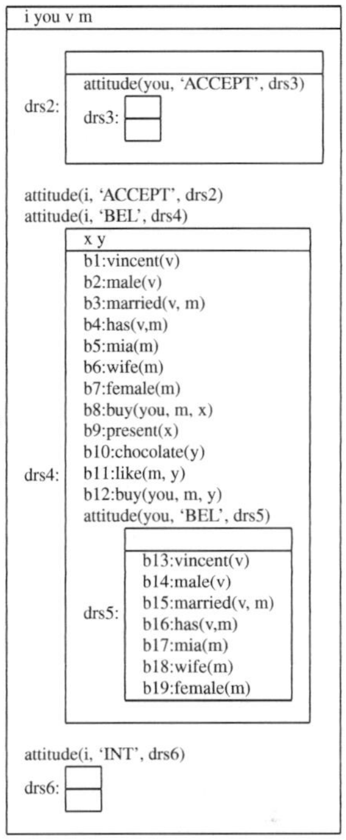

Figure 5: Speaker Initial State

5 Conclusion

This paper has introduced a pragmatic view of presupposition both in terms of givenness and the effects agents' cognitive states have on formulating presupposition. To introduce this pragmatic view of presupposition into DRT, some pragmatic constraints have been formulated and demonstrated by way of example. In addition, an implementation of these pragmatic constraints on presupposition has been introduced into the extended DRT representation formulated by Al-Raheb (2005).

References

Al-Raheb, Y. 2005. *Speaker/Hearer Representation in a Discourse Representation Theory Model of Presupposition: A Computational-Linguistic Approach.* Phd. University of East Anglia.

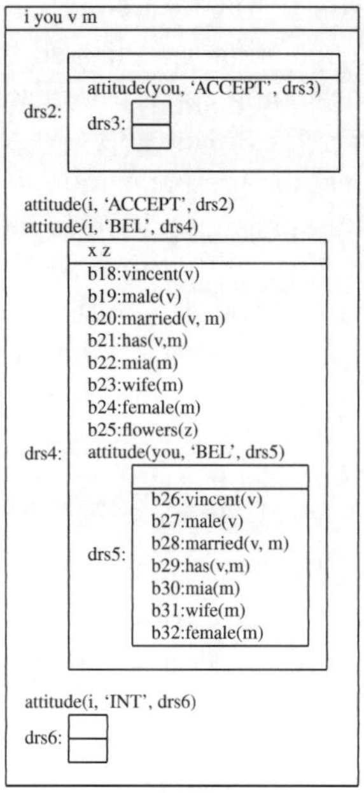

Figure 6: Hearer Initial State

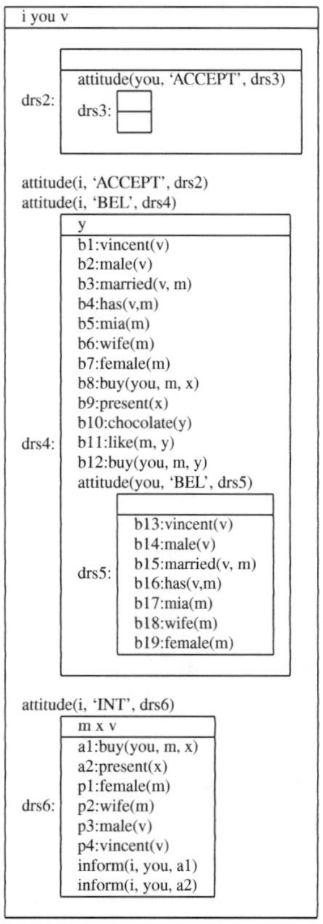

Figure 7: Speaker Generation: After S1

Geurts, B. 1999. *Presuppositions and Pronouns: Current Research in the Semantics/ Pragmatics Interface*. Oxford: Elsevier.

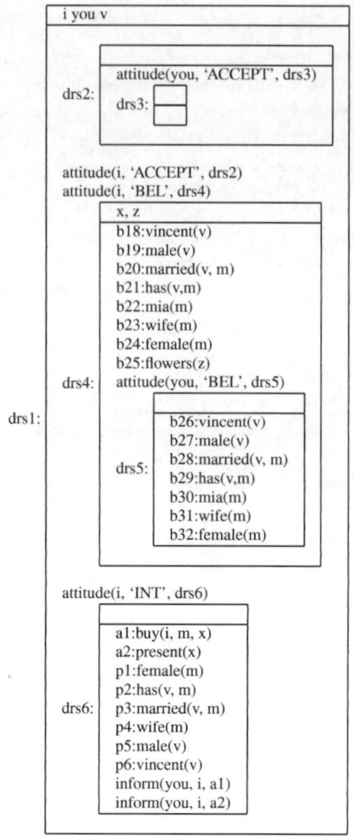

Figure 8: Hearer Recognition: After S1

Grice, P. 1989. *Studies in the Way of Words*. Cambridge, MA: Harvard University Press.

Lambrecht, K. 1994. *Information Structure and Sentence Form: Topic, Focus and the Mental Representations of Discourse Referents*. Cambridge: Cambridge University Press.

Levinson, S. 1983. *Pragmatics*. Cambridge: Cambridge University Press.

Simons, M. 2003. 'Presupposition and Accommodation: Understanding the Stalnakerian Picture'. *Philosophical Studies* 112, pp. 251–278.

Stalnaker, R. 2002. 'Common ground'. *Linguistics and Philosophy* 25(5-6), pp. 701–721.

van der Sandt, R. and Geurts, B. 1991. 'Presupposition, Anaphora, and Lexical Content'. In: O. Herzog and C.-R. Rollinger (Eds.). *Text Understanding in LILOG*. pp. 259–296. Berlin, Heidelberg: Springer Verlag.

van der Sandt, R. 1992. 'Presupposition Projection as Anaphora Resolution'. *Journal of Semantics* 9, pp. 333–377.

Werth, P. 1999. *Text Worlds: Representing Conceptual Space in Discourse*. New York: Longman.

Coupling a Linguistic Formalism and a Script Language

Claude Roux
Xerox Research Centre Europe/ 6,
chemin de Maupertuis, 38240 Meylan,
France
Claude.roux@xrce.xerox.com

Abstract

This article presents a novel syntactic parser architecture, in which a linguistic formalism can be enriched with all sorts of constraints, included extra-linguistic ones, thanks to the seamless coupling of the formalism with a programming language.

1 Introduction

The utilization of constraints in natural language parsers (see Blache and Balfourier,2001 or Tapanainen and Järvinen , 1994) is central to most systems today. However, these constraints are often limited to purely linguistic features, such as linearity or dependency relations between categories within a given syntactic tree. Most linguistic formalisms have been created with the sole purpose of extracting linguistic information from bits and pieces of text. They usually use a launch and forget strategy, where a text is analyzed according to local constraints, displayed and then discarded to make room for the next block of text. These parsers take each sentence as an independent input, on which grammar rules are applied together with constraints. However, no sentence is independent of a text, and no text is really independent of extra-linguistic information. In order to assess correctly the phrase *President Bush*, we need to know that *Bush* is a proper name, whose function is "President". *Washington* can be a town, a state, the name of a famous president, but also the name of an actor. Moreover, the analysis of a sentence is never an independent process, if *President Bush* is found in a text, the reference to *president*, later in the document will be related to this phrase.

These problems are certainly not new and a dense literature has been written about how to better deal with these issues. However, most solutions rely on formalism enrichments with solutions "engraved in stone", that makes it difficult to adapt a grammar to new domains (see Declerck, 2002, or Roux, 2004), even though they use XML representation or database to store huge amounts of extra-linguistic information. The interpretation of these data is intertwined into the very fabric of the parser and requires deep modifications to use new sources with a complete different DTD.

Of course, there are many other ways to solve these problems. For instance, in the case of languages such as Prolog or Lisp, the grammar formalism is often indistinguishable from the programming language itself. For these parsers, the querying of external information is easily solved as grammar rules can be naturally augmented with non-linguistic procedures that are written in the same language. In other cases, when the parser is independent from any specific programming languages, the problem can prove difficult to solve. The formalism can of course be augmented with new instructions to tackle the querying of external information. However the time required to enrich the parser language may not be worth the effort, as the development of a complete new instruction set is a heavy and complex task that is loosely related to linguistic parser programming.

We propose in this article a new way of building natural language parsers, with the coupling of a script language with an already rich linguistic formalism.

2 Scripting

The system we describe in this article mix a natural language parser, namely Xerox Incremental Parser (XIP hereafter, see Aït-Mohktar et al., 2002, Roux, 1999) with a scripting language, in our case Python. The interaction of a grammar with scripting instructions is almost as old as

Proceedings of the 3rd Workshop on Constraints and Language Processing (CSLP-06), pages 33–40,
Sydney, July 2006. ©2006 Association for Computational Linguistics

computational linguistics. Pereira and Shieber for instance, in their book: Prolog and Natural Language Processing (see Pereira and Shieber, 1987) already suggested mixing grammar rules with extra-linguistic information. This mélange was made possible thanks to the homogeneity between grammar rules and the external code, written in both cases in the same programming language. However, these programming languages are not exactly tuned to do linguistic analyses; they are often slow and cumbersome. Moreover, they blur the boundary between program and grammar rules, as the programming language is both the algorithm language and the rule language. Allen (see Allen, 1994) proposes a different approach in his TRAINS Parsing system. The grammar formalism is independent to a certain extent from the implementation language, which is LISP in this case. However, since the grammar is translated into a LISP program, it is easy for a linguist to specialize the generated rules with external LISP procedures. Nevertheless, the grammar formalism remains very close to LISP data description, which makes the grammar rules somewhat difficult to read.

The other solution, which is usually favored by computational linguists, is to store the external information in databases, which are accessed with some pre-defined instructions and translated into linguistic features. For instance (see Declerk, 2002 or Roux, 2004), the external information is presented as an XML document whose DTD is defined once and for all. This DTD is then enriched with extra-linguistic information that a parser can exploit to guide rule application. This method alleviates the necessity of a complex interaction mechanism between the parser and its external data sources. The XPath language is used to query this document in order to retrieve salient information at parsing time, which is then translated into local linguistic features. However, only static information can be exploited, as these XML databases must be built beforehand.

Similar mechanisms have also been proposed in other architectures to help heterogeneous linguistic modules to communicate through a common XML interface (see Cunningham et al.,2002, Blache and Guénot , 2003). These architectures are very powerful as they connect together tools that only need to comply with a common input/output DTD. Specialized Java modules can then be written which are applied to intermediate representations to add their own touch of extra-linguistic data. Since, the intermediate representation is an XML document, the number of possible enrichments is almost limitless, as each module will only extract from this document the XML markup tags that it is designed to handle. However, since XML is by nature furiously verbose, the overall system might be very slow as it might spend a large amount of time translating external XML representation into internal representations.

Furthermore, applications that require natural language processing also have different purposes, different needs. They may require a shallow output, such as a simple tokenization with a whiff of tagging, or a much deeper analysis. Syntactic parsing is usually integrated as a black box into these architectures, with little control left over the grammar execution, control which nevertheless might prove very important in many cases. An XML document, for instance, often contains some specific markup tags to identify a title, a section or author name. If the parser is given some indications about the input, it could be guided through the grammar maze to favor these rules that are better suited to analyze a title for example.

Finally, syntactic parsing, when it is limited to lexical information, often fails to assess correctly some ambiguous relations. Thus, the only way to deal with PP-attachment or anaphoric pronoun antecedents is to use both previous analyses and external information. However, most syntactic parsers are often ill geared to link with external modules. The formalism is engraved into a C program as in Link Grammar (see Grinberg et al.,1995) or as in Sylex (see Constant, 1995) which offers little or no opening to the rest of the world, as it is mainly designed to accomplish one unique task. We will show how the seamless integration of a script language into the very fabric of the formalism simplifies the task of keeping track of previous analyses together with the use of external sources of data.

3 Xerox Incremental Parser (XIP)

The XIP engine has been developed by a research team in computational linguistics at the Xerox Research Centre Europe (see Aït-Mokhtar et al., 2001). It has been designed from the beginning to follow a strictly incremental strategy, where rules apply one after the other. There is only one analysis path that is followed for a given linguistic unit (phrase, sentence or even paragraph): the failure of a rule does not prevent the whole analysis from continuing to completion. Since the system never backtracks on any rules, XIP cannot propel itself into a combinatorial explosion.

XIP can be divided into two main components:

- A component that builds a chunk tree on the basis of lexical nodes.
- A component that creates functions or dependencies that connect together distant nodes from the chunk tree.

The central goal of this parser is the extraction of dependencies. A dependency is a function that connects together distant nodes within a chunk tree. The system constructs a dependency between two nodes, if these two nodes are in a specific configuration within the chunk tree or if a specific set of dependencies has already been extracted for some of these nodes (see Hagege and Roux, 2002). The notion of constraint embedded in XIP is both configurational and Boolean. The configuration part is based on tree regular rules which express constraints over node configuration, while the Boolean constraints are expressed over dependencies.

3.1 Three Level of Analysis

The parsing is done in three different stages:

- Part-of-speech disambiguation and chunking.
- Dependency Extraction between words on the basis of sub-tree patterns over the chunk sequence.
- Combination of those dependencies with Boolean operators to generate new dependencies, or to modify or delete existing dependencies.

3.2 The Different Steps of Analysis

Below is an example of how a sentence is parsed. We present a little grammar, written in the XIP formalism, together with the output yielded by these rules.

Example
The chunking rules produce a chunk tree.

In a first stage, chunking rules are applied and the following chunk tree is built for this sentence.
Below is a small XIP grammar that can analyze the above example:

```
1> AP = Adj.
2> NP @= Det,(AP),(Noun),Noun.
3> FV= verb.
4> SC= NP,FV.
```

Each rule is associated with a layer number, which defines the order in which the rules must be executed.
If this grammar is applied to the above sentence, the result is the following:

```
TOP{SC{NP{The AP{chunking} rules}
    FV{produce}}
  NP{a chunk tree}
  .}
```

TOP is a node that is automatically created, once all chunking rules have applied, to transform this sequence of chunks into a tree.
(The "@" denotes a longest match strategy. The rule is then applied to the longest sequence of categories found in the linguistic unit)

The next step consists of extracting some basic dependencies from this tree. These dependencies are obtained with some very basic rules that only connect nodes that occur in a specific sub-tree configuration.

```
SUBJ(produce,rules)
OBJ(produce,tree)
```

SUBJ is a subject relation, which has been extracted with the following rule:

```
| NP{?*, noun#1}, FV{?*,verb#2}|
  SUBJ(#2,#1).
```

This rule links together the noun and the verb respectively the sub-nodes of a NP and a VP that are next to each other. The "{…}" denotes a pattern over sub-nodes.

Other rules may then be applied to this output, to add or modify existing dependencies.

```
if (SUBJ(#1,#2) & OBJ(#1,#3))
 TRIPLET(#2,#1,#3).
```

For instance, the above rule will generate a three slot dependency *TRIPLET* with the nodes extracted from the subject and object dependencies. If we apply this rule to our previous example, we will create: TRIPLET(rules,produce,tree).

3.3 Script Language

The utilization of a script language deeply ingrained into the parser fabric might sound like a pure technical gadget with very little influence on parsing theories. However, the development of a parser often poses some very trivial problems, which we can sum up in the three questions below:

- How can we use previous analyses?
- How do we access external information?
- How do we control the grammar from an embedding application?

Usually, the answer for each of these questions leads to three different implementations, as none of these problems seem to have any connections whatsoever. Their only common point seems to be some extra-programming into the parser engine. If a grammar and a parser are both written in the same programming language, the problem is relatively simple to solve. However, if the grammar is written in a formalism specifically designed for linguistic analysis interpreted with a linguistic compiler (as it is the case for XIP), then any new features that would implement some of these instructions translate into a modification of the parsing engine itself. However, one cannot expand the parser engine forever. The solution that has been chosen in XIP is to develop a script language, which linguists can use to enrich the original grammatical formalism with new instructions.

3.4 First attempts

The first attempts to add scripting instructions to XIP consisted in enriching the grammar with numerical and string variables together with some instructions to handle these values. For instance, it is possible in XIP to declare a string variable, to instantiate it with the lemma value of a syntactic node and to apply some string modifications upon it. However, the development of such a script language, however useful it proved, became closer and closer to a general-purpose programming language, which XIP was not designed to be. The task of developing a full-fledged programming language with a large instruction set is a complex ongoing process, which has little connection with parsing theories. Nevertheless, there was a need for such an addendum, which led the development team to link XIP with Python, whose own ongoing development is backed up by thousands of dedicated computer scientists.

3.5 Python

Scripting languages have been around for a very long time. Thus Perl and Awk have been part of the Unix OS for at least twenty years. Python is already an old language, in computational time scale. It has been central to the Linux environment for more than ten years. Most of the basic installation procedures are written in that language. It has also been ported to a variety of platforms such as Windows or Mac OS. The language syntax is close to C, but lacks type verification. However, the language is thoroughly documented and a large quantity of specialized libraries is available. Python has also been chosen because of the simplicity of its API, which allows programmers to link easily a Python engine to their own application or to enlarge the language with new libraries. The other reason of this choice, over for instance a more conventional language such as C or Java is the fact that it is an interpreted language. A XIP grammar is a set of text files, which are all compiled on the fly in memory every time the parser is run. It stems from this choice that any addenda to this grammar should be written in a language that is also compiled on the fly. In this way, the new instructions can be developed in parallel with the grammar and immediately put in test. It also simplifies the non-trivial task of debugging a complete grammar as any modifications on any parts of the grammar can be immediately experimented together with the python script.
We have produced two different versions of the XIP-python parsing engine.

3.6 Python Embedded within XIP

We have linked the python engine to XIP, which allows us to call and execute python scripts from within the parsing engine. In this case, a grammar rule can call a python script to verify specific conditions. The python scripts are then appended to the grammar itself. These scripts have full access to all linguistic objects constructed so far. XIP is the master program with python scripts being triggered by grammar rules.

3.7 XIP as a Python Library

We have created a specific XIP library which can be freely imported in python. In this case, the XIP library exports a basic API, compliant with the python programming interface, which allows python developers to benefit from the XIP engine. The XIP results are then returned as python objects. Since the purpose in this article is to show how a grammar formalism can be enriched with new instructions, we will mainly concentrate on the first point.

3.8 Interfacing Python and a XIP grammar

A XIP grammar mainly handles syntactic nodes, features, categories, and dependencies. In order to be efficient, a Python script, called from a XIP grammar, should have access to all this information in a simple and natural way. The notion of procedure has already been added to the XIP formalism. They can be used in any sort of rule.

Example

```
if (subject(#1,#2) & TestNode(#1))
   ambiguous(#1).
```

The above rule tests the existence of a subject dependency and will use the TestNode procedure to check some properties of the #1 node. If all these conditions are true, then a new dependency: *ambiguous* is created with #1 as parameter.

3.9 Interface

The *TestNode* procedure is declared in a XIP grammar in the following way:

Example

```
Python: //XIP field name
   TestNode(#1). //the XIP procedure name, with
                   XIP parameter style.

   //All that follows is in Python
   def TestNode(node):
   ...
```

The only constraint is that the XIP procedure name (*TestNode*) should also have been implemented as a Python procedure. If this Python procedure is missing, then the grammar compilation fails.

The system works as a very simple linker, where the code integrity is verified to the presence of common names in XIP and Python.

However, the next step, which consists in translating XIP data into Python data, is done at runtime.

XIP recognizes many different sorts of data, which can all be transmitted to a Python script, such as syntactic nodes, dependencies, integer variables, string variables, or even vector variables. Each of these data is then translated into simple Python variables. However, the syntactic nodes and the dependencies are not directly transformed into Python objects; we simply propagate them into the Python code as integers. Each node and each dependency has a unique index, which simplifies the task of sharing parameters between XIP and Python.

3.10 XIP API

Python procedures have access to all internal parsing data through a specific API. This API consists of a dozen instructions, which can be called anywhere in the Python code. For instance, XIP provides Python instructions to return a node or a dependency object on the basis of its index. We have implemented the Python XipNode class, with the following fields:

```
class XipNode
    index        #the unique index of the node
    POS          #the part of speech
    Lemma        #a vector of possible lemmas
                 for the node
    Surface      #the surface form as it ap
                 pears in the sentence
    features     #a vector of attribute-value
                 features
    leftoffset,rightoffset #the text offsets
    next,previous,parent,child    # indexes
```

A XipNode object is automatically created when the object creator is called with the node index as parameter. We can also travel through the syntactic tree, thanks to the *next, previous, parent, child* indexes that are provided by this class.

There is a big difference between using this API and exploiting the regular output of a syntactic parser. Since the Python procedures are called at runtime from the grammar, they have full access to the on-going linguistic data. Second, the selection of syntactic nodes on which to apply Python procedures is done at *the grammar level*, which means that the access of specific nodes is done through the parsing engine itself, without any need to duplicate any sorts of tree operators, which would be mandatory in the case of a Java, XML or C++ object. Finally, the memory footprint is only limited to the nodes that are requested by the application, there is no need to reduplicate the whole linguistic data structure. The memory footprint reduction also has the effect of speeding up the execution.

3.11 Other Basic Instructions

XIP provides the following Python instructions:

- **XipDependency(index)** builds a XipDependency object.
- **nodeset(POS)** returns a vector of node indices corresponding to a POS: *nodeset("noun")*
- **dependencyset(POS)** returns a vector of dependency indices corresponding to a dependency name: *dependencyset("SUBJECT")*
- **dependencyonfirstnode(n)** returns a vector of dependency indices, whose first parameter is the node index *n: dependencyonfirstnode(12)*

These basic instructions make it possible for a Python script to access all internal XIP data at any stages.

3.12 An Example

Let us define the Python code of *TestNbSenses*, which checks whether a verbal node is highly ambiguous according to WordNet. As a demonstration, a verb will be said to be highly ambiguous if the number of its senses is larger than 10.

```
def TestNbSenses(i):
   n=XipNode(i)
   senses=N[n.lemma].getSenses()
   if len(senses)>=10:
     return 1
   return 0
```

We can now use this procedure in a syntactic rule to test the ambiguity of a verb in order to guide the grammar:

```
if (subject(#1,#2) & TestNbSenses(#1))
         ambiguous(#1).
```

The dependency *ambiguous* will be created for a verbal node, if this verb is highly ambiguous.

4 Back to the Initial Questions

The questions we wish to answer are the following:

- How can we use previous analyses?
- How do we access external information?
- How do we control the grammar from an embedding application?

We have shown in the previous section how new instructions could be easily defined and thus become part of the XIP formalism. These instructions are mapped to a Python program which offers all we need to answer the above questions.

4.1 How can we use previous analyses?

Since, we have a full access to the internal linguistic representation of XIP, we can store whatever data we might find useful for a given task. For instance, we could decide to count the number of time a word has been detected in the course of parsing. This could be implemented with a Python dictionary variable.

```
Python:
   countword(#1).
   getcount(#1).
   ...
```

The first procedure *countword* receives a node index as input. It translates it into a XipNode, and it uses the lemma as an entry for the Python dictionary *wordcounter*. At the end of the process, *wordcounter* contains a list of words with their number of occurrences. The second procedure implements a simple test which returns the number of time a word has been found. It returns 0, if it is an unknown word.
The grammar rule below is used to count words:

```
|Noun#1| {
        countword(#1);
}
```

The instruction *|noun#1|* automatically loops between all *noun* nodes.
The rule below is used to test if a word has already been found:

```
if (subject(#1,#2) & getcount(#2)) ...
```

4.2 How do we access external information?

We have already given an example with WordNet. Thanks to the large number of libraries available, a Python script can benefit from WordNet information. It can also connect to a variety of databases such as MySQL, which also allows a grammar to query a database for specific data.
For instance, we could store in a database verb-noun couples that have been extracted from a

large corpus. Then, at runtime, a grammar could check whether a certain verb and a certain noun have already been found together in another document.

Example

Python:
TestCouple(#1,#2).

```
def TestCouple(v,n):
   noun=XipNode(n)
   verb=XipNode(v)
   cmd="select * from couples where "
   cmd+="verb="+verb.lemma+"
   cmd+=" and noun="+noun.lemma+";"
   nb=mysql.execute(cmd)
   return nb
```

In the XIP grammar:

```
|FV{verb#1},PP{prep,NP{noun#2}}|
  if (TestCouple(#1,#2))
     Complement(#1,#2).
```

If we have a *verb* followed by a *PP*, then if we have already found in a previous analysis a link between the *verb* and the *noun* embedded in the *PP*, we create a dependency *Complement* over the *verb* and the *noun*.

4.3 How do we control the grammar from an embedding application?

Since a Python script can exploit any sort of input, from text files to databases; it becomes relatively simple to implement a simple Python procedure that blocks the execution of certain grammar rules. If we examine the above example, we can see how the grammar execution can be modified by an external calling program. For instance, the selection of a different database will have a strong influence on how dependencies are constructed.

5 Expression Power

The main goal of this article is to describe a way to articulate no-linguistic constraints with a dedicated linguistic formalism. The notion of constraint in this perspective does not only apply to purely linguistic properties such as category order or dependency building constraints; it is enlarged to encompass properties that are rarely taken into account in syntactic theories. It should be noted, however, that if most theories are designed to apply to a single sentence, nothing prevents these formalisms to benefit from extra-linguistic data through a complex feature system that would encode the sentence context. How these features are instantiated is nevertheless out the realm of these theories. The originality of our system lies in the fact that we intertwine from the beginning these constraints into the fabric of the formalism. Since any rules can be governed by a Boolean expression, which in turn can accept any Boolean python functions, it becomes feasible to define a formalism in which a constraint is no longer reduced to only linguistic data, but to any properties that a full-fledged programming language can allow. Thus, any rule can be constrained during its application with complex constraints which are implemented as a python script.

Example

pythontest is a generic Boolean python function, which any XIP rules can embed within its own set of constraints.

Below are some examples of XIP rules, which are constrained with this generic python function. A constraint in XIP is introduced with the keyword "*if*".

- A chunking rule:

PP = prep, NP#1, if (*pythontest*(#1)).

- A dependency rule:

if (subject(#1,#2) & *pythontest*(#1)) …

However, since any rule might be constrained with an external process it should be noted that this system can no longer be described as a pure linguistic parser. Its expression power largely exceeds what is usually expected from a syntactic formalism.

6 Implementation Examples

We have successfully used Python in our grammars in two different applications so far. The first implementation consists of a script that is called at the end of any sentence analysis to store the results in a MySQL database. Since the saving is done with a Python program, it is very simple to modify this script to store only information that is salient to a particular application. In this respect, the maintenance of such a script is much simpler and much flexible than its C++ or Java counterpart. The storage is also done at runtime which limits the amount of data kept in memory.

The second example is the implementation of a co-reference system (Salah Aït-Mohktar to appear), which uses Python as a backup language to keep a specific representation of linguistic information that is used at the end of the analysis to link together pronouns and their antecedents. Once again, this program could have been created in C++ or Java, using the C++ or the Java XIP API, however, the development of such a system in python benefits from the simplicity of the language itself and its direct bridge to internal XIP representation.

7 Conclusion

The integration of a linguistic parser into an application has always posed some tricky problems. First, the grammar, whether it has been compiled into an external library or run through an interpreter, often works as a black box, which allows little or no possibility of interfering with the internal execution. Second, the output is usually frozen into one single object which forces the calling applications to perform format translation afterward. In many systems (Cunningham et al.,2002, Grinberg et al., 1995), the output is often a large, complex object, or a large XML document. This has an impact on both memory footprint (these objects might be very large) and the analysis speed as the system must reimplement some tree operators to traverse these objects. Thereby, the automatic extraction of all nodes that share a common property on the basis of these objects requires some cumbersome programming, when this could be more elegantly handled through the linguistic formalism. Third, the use of extra-linguistic information often imposes a modification of the parsing engine itself, which prevents developers from switching quickly between heterogeneous data sources. For a long time, linguistic formalisms have been conceived as specialized theoretical languages with little if no algorithmic possibilities. However, today, the use of syntactic parsers in large applications triggers the need for more than just pure linguistic description. For all these reasons, the integration of a script language as part of the formalism seems a reasonable solution, as it will transform dedicated linguistic formalisms to linguistically driven programming languages.

Reference

Gazdar G., Klein E., Pullum G., Sag A. I., 1985. *Generalized Phrase Structure Grammar,* Blackwell, Cambridge Mass., Harvard University Press.

Pereira F. and S. Shieber, 1987. *Prolog and Natural Language Analysis,* CSLI, Chicago University Press.

Allen J. F, 1994. *TRAINS Parsing System,* Natural Language Understanding, Second Ed., chapters 3,4,5.

Tapanainen P., Järvinen T. 1994. *Syntactic analysis of natural language using linguistic rules and corpus-based patterns*, Proceedings of the 15th conference on Computational linguistics, Kyoto, Japan, pages: 629-634.

Constant P. 1995. *L'analyseur Linguistique SYLEX*, 5 ème école d'été du CNET.

Grinberg D., Lafferty John, Sleator D., 1995. *A robust parsing algorithm for link grammars,* Carnegie Mellon University Computer Science technical report CMU-CS-95-125, also Proceedings of the Fourth International Workshop on Parsing Technologies, Prague, September, 1995.

Fellbaum C., 1998. *WordNet: An Electronic Lexical Database*, Rider University and Princeton University, Cambridge, MA: The MIT Press (Language, speech, and communication series), 1998, xxii+423 pp; hardbound, ISBN 0-262-06197-X.

Roux C. 1999. *Phrase-Driven Parser,*Proceedings of VEXTALL 99, Venezia, San Servolo, V.I.U. - 22-24.

Blache P., Balfourier J.-M., 2001. *Property Grammars: a Flexible Constraint-Based Approach to Parsing*, in proceedings of *IWPT-2001*.

Aït-Mokhtar S., Chanod J-P., Roux C., 2002. *Robustness beyond shallowness incremental dependency parsing*, NLE Journal, 2002.

Hagège C., Roux C.,2002. *A Robust And Flexible Platform for Dependency Extraction*, in proceedings of LREC 2002.

Declerck T. 2002, *A set of tools for integrating linguistic and non-linguistic information*, Proceedings of SAAKM.

H. Cunningham, D. Maynard, K. Bontcheva, V. Tablan.,2002. *GATE: A Framework and Graphical Development Environment for Robust NLP Tools and Applications*, Proceedings of the 40th Anniversary Meeting of the Association for Computational Linguistics (ACL'02), Philadelphia, July 2002.

Blache P., Guénot M-L. 2003. *Flexible Corpus Annotation with Property Grammars*, BulTreeBank Project

Roux C., 2004. *Une Grammaire XML,* TALN Conference, Fez, Morocco, April, 19-22, 2004.

[Python] http://www.python.org/

Capturing Disjunction in Lexicalization with Extensible Dependency Grammar

Jorge Marques Pelizzoni
ICMC - Univ. de São Paulo - Brazil
Langue & Dialogue - LORIA - France
Jorge.Pelizzoni@loria.fr

Maria das Graças Volpe Nunes
ICMC - Univ. de São Paulo - Brazil
gracan@icmc.usp.br

Abstract

In spite of its potential for bidirectionality, Extensible Dependency Grammar (XDG) has so far been used almost exclusively for parsing. This paper represents one of the first steps towards an XDG-based integrated generation architecture by tackling what is arguably the most basic among generation tasks: lexicalization. Herein we present a constraint-based account of *disjunction* in lexicalization, i.e. a way to enable an XDG grammar to generate all paraphrases — along the lexicalization axis, of course — realizing a given input semantics. Our model is (i) efficient, yielding strong propagation, (ii) modular and (iii) favourable to synergy inasmuch as it allows collaboration between modules, notably semantics and syntax. We focus on constraints ensuring well-formedness and completeness and avoiding over-redundancy.

1 Introduction

In text generation the term *lexicalization* (Reiter and Dale, 2000) refers to deciding which among a choice of potentially applicable lexical items realizing a given intended meaning are actually going to take part in a generated utterance. It can be regarded as a general, necessary generation task — especially if one agrees that the term *task* does not necessarily imply pipelining — and remarkably pervasive at that. For instance, even though the realization of such a phrase as "a ballerina" owes much to *referring expression generation*, a complementary task, it is still a matter of lexicalization whether to prioritize that specific phrase over all its possible legitimate alternates, e.g. "a female dancer", "a dancing woman" or "a dancing female person". However, prior to the statement of prioritizing criteria or selection preferences and rather as the very substratum thereto, the ultimate matter of lexicalization is exactly alternation, choice — in one word, *disjunction*.

Given the combinatorial nature of language and specifically the interchangeability of lexical items yielding hosts of possible valid solutions to one same instance lexicalization task, disjunction may well become a major source of (combinatorial) complexity. Our subject matter in this paper is solely disjunction in lexicalization as a basis for more advanced lexicalization models, and our purpose is precisely to describe a constraint-based model that *(i) captures the disjunctive potential of lexicalization*, i.e. allows the generation of all mutually paraphrasing solutions (according to a given language model) to any given lexicalization task, *(ii) ensures well-formedness*, especially ruling out over-redundancy (such as found in "∗a dancing female dancer/ballerina/woman") and syntactic anomalies ("∗a dancer woman"), and does so *(iii) modularly*, in that not only are concerns neatly separated (e.g. semantics vs. syntax), but also solutions are reusable, and future extensions, likely to be developed with no change to current modules, *(iv) efficiently*, having an implementation yielding strong propagation and thus prone to keep complexity at acceptable levels, and *(v) synergicly*, inasmuch as it promotes the interplay between modules (namely syntax and semantics) and seems compatible with the concept of integrated generation architectures (Reiter and Dale, 2000), i.e. those in which tasks are not executed in pipeline, but are rather interleaved so as to avoid failed or suboptimal choices during search.

We build upon the Extensible Dependency Grammar (XDG) (Debusmann et al., 2004b; Debusmann et al., 2004a; Debusmann et al., 2005) model and its CP implementation in Oz (Van Roy and Haridi, 2004), namely the XDG Development Toolkit[1] (XDK) (Debusmann et al., 2004c).

[1] http://www.ps.uni-sb.de/~rade/xdg.

Proceedings of the 3rd Workshop on Constraints and Language Processing (CSLP-06), pages 41–50,
Sydney, July 2006.

In fact, all those appealing goals of modularity, efficiency and synergy are innate to XDG and the XDK, and our work can most correctly be regarded as the very first attempts at equipping XDG for generation and fulfilling its bidirectional promise.

The paper proceeds as follows. Section 2 provides background information on XDG and the XDK. Section 3 motivates our lexicalization disjunction model and describes it both intuitively and formally, while Section 4 presents implementation highlights, assuming familiarity with the XDK and focusing on the necessary additions and modifications to it, as well as discussing performance. Finally, in Section 5 we conclude and discuss future work.

2 Extensible Dependency Grammar

An informal overview of XDG's core concepts is in order; for a formal description of XDG, however, see (Debusmann and Smolka, 2006; Debusmann et al., 2005). Strictly speaking, XDG is not a grammatical framework, but rather a description language over finite labelled multigraphs that happens to show very convenient properties for the modeling of natural language, among which a remarkable reconciliation between monostratality, on one side, and modularity and extensibility, on the other.

Most of XDG's strengths stem from its *multi-dimensional metaphor* (see Fig. 1), whereby an (holistic or multidimensional) XDG analysis consists of a set of concurrent, synchronized, complementary, mutually constraining one-dimensional analyses, each of which is itself a *graph* sharing the same set of nodes as the other analyses, but having its own type or **dimension**, i.e., its own edge label and lexical feature types and its own well-formedness constraints. In other words, each 1D analysis has a nature and interpretation of its own, associates each node with one respective instance of a data type of its own (lexical features) and establishes its own relations/edges between nodes using labels and principles of its own.

That might sound rather autistic at first, but the 1D components of an XDG analysis interact in fact. It is exactly their sharing one same set of nodes, whose sole intrinsic property is identity, that provides the substratum for interdimensional communication, or rather, *mutual constraining*.

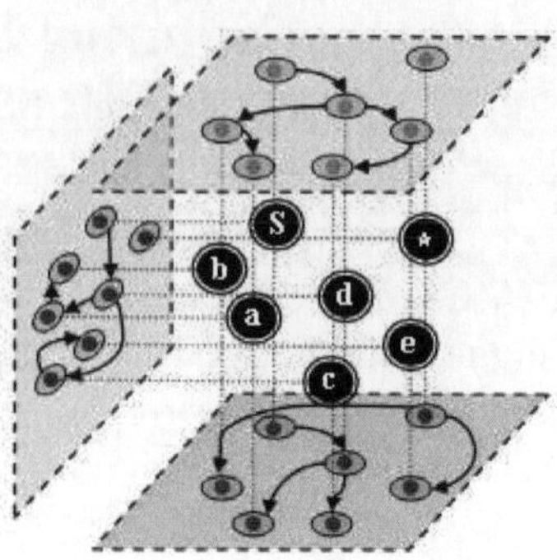

Figure 1: Three concurrent one-dimensional analyses. It is the sharing of one same set of nodes that co-relates and synchronizes them into one holistic XDG analysis.

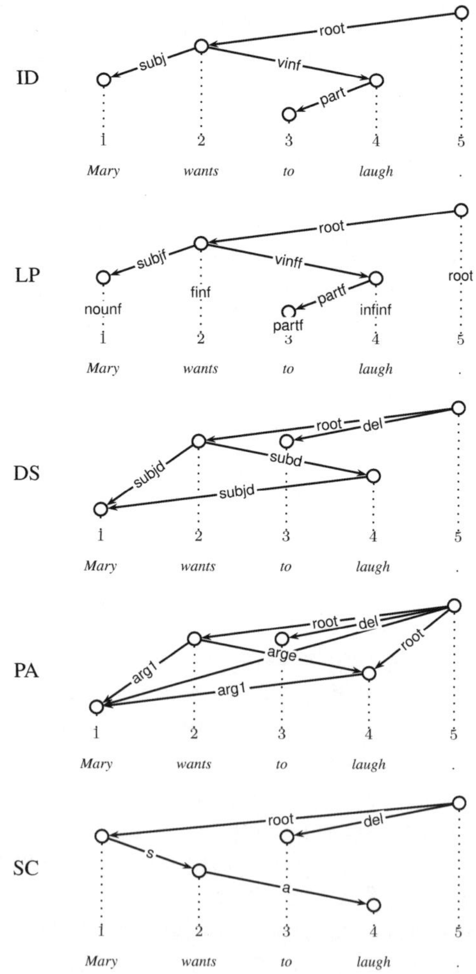

Figure 2: A 5D XDG analysis for "Mary wants to laugh." according to grammar *Chorus.ul* deployed with the XDK

html

That is chiefly achieved by means of two devices, namely: multidimensional principles and lexical synchronization.

Multidimensional principles. Principles are reusable, usually parametric constraint predicates used to define grammars and their dimensions. Those posing constraints between two or more 1D analyses are said **multidimensional**. For example, the XDK library provides a host of *linking principles*, one of whose main applications is to regulate the relationship between semantic arguments and syntactic roles according to lexical specifications. The framework allows lexical entries to contain features of the type $lab(D_1) \rightarrow \{lab(D_2)\}$, i.e. mappings from edge labels in dimension D_1 to sets of edge labels in D_2. Therefore, lexical entries specifying $\{pat \rightarrow \{subj\}\}$ might be characteristic of unaccusative verbs, while those with $\{agt \rightarrow \{subj\}\,,\ pat \rightarrow \{obj\}\}$ would suit a class of transitive ones. Linking principles pose constraints taking this kind of features into account.

Lexical synchronization. The lexicon component in XDG is specified in two steps: first, each dimension declares its own lexicon entry type; next, once all dimensions have been declared, lexicon entries are provided, each specifying the values for features on all dimensions. Finally, at runtime it is required of well-formed analyses that there should be at least one valid assignment of lexicon entries to nodes such that all principles are satisfied. In other words, every node must be assigned a lexicon entry that *simultaneously* satisfies all principles on all dimensions, for which reason the lexicon is said to synchronize all 1D components of an XDG analysis. Lexical synchronization is a major source of propagation.

Figure 2 presents a sample 5D XDG analysis involving the most standard dimensions in XDG practice and jargon, namely **(i) PA**, capturing predicate argument structure; **(ii) SC**, capturing the scopes of quantifiers; **(iii) DS**, for *deep syntax*, i.e. syntactic structure modulo control and raising phenomena; **(iv) ID**, for *immediate dominance* in surface syntax (as opposed to DS); and **(v) LP**, for *linear precedence*, i.e. a structure tightly related to ID working as a substratum for constraints on the order of utterance of words. In fact, among these dimensions LP is the only one actually to involve a concept of order. PA and DS, in turn, are the only ones not constrained to be trees, but directed acyclic graphs instead. Further details on the meaning of all these dimensions, as well as the interactions between them, would be beyond the scope of this paper and have been dealt with elsewhere. From Section 3 on we shall focus on PA and, to a lesser extent, the dimension with which it interfaces directly: DS.

Emulating deletion. Figure 2 also illustrates the rather widespread technique of deletion, there applied to infinitival “to” on dimensions DS, PA, and SC. As XDG is an eminently monostratal and thus non-transformational framework, “deletion” herein refers to an emulation thereof. According to this technique, whenever a node has but one incoming edge with a reserved label, say del, on dimension D it is considered as virtually deleted on D. In addition, one artificial root node is postulated from which emerge as many del edges as required on all dimensions. The trick also comes in handy when tackling, for instance, multiword expressions (Debusmann, 2004), which involve worthy syntactic nodes that conceptually have no semantic counterparts.

3 Modelling Lexicalization Disjunction in XDG

Generation input. Having revised the basics of XDG, it is worth mentioning that so far it has been used mostly for parsing, in which case the input type is usually rather straightforward, namely typewritten sentences or possibly other text units. Model creation is also very simple in parsing and consists of (i) creating exactly one node for each input token, all nodes being instances of one single homogeneous feature structure type automatically inferred from the grammar definition, (ii) making each node select from all the lexical entries indexed by its respective token, (iii) posing constraints automatically generated from the principles found in the grammar definition and (iv) deterministically assigning values to the order-related variables in nodes so as to reflect the actual order of tokens in input.

As concerns generation, things are not so clear, though. For a start, take input, which usually varies across applications and systems, not to mention the fact that representability and computability of meaning in general are open issues. Model creation should follow closely, as it is a direct function of input. Notwithstanding, we can to some extent and advantage tell what generation input is not. Under the hypothesis of an XDG-based generation system tackling lexicalization, input is not likely to contain some direct representation of fully specified PA analyses, much though this is usually regarded as a satisfactory output for a parsing system (!). What happens here is that *generating* an input PA analysis would presuppose lexicalization having already been carried out. In other words, PA analyses accounting for e.g. "a ballerina" and "a dancing female human being" have absolutely nothing to do with each other whereas what we wish is exactly to feed input allowing both realizations. Therefore, PA analyses are themselves part of generation output and are acceptable as parsing output inasmuch as "de-lexicalization" is considered a trivial task, which is not necessarily true, however.

Although our system still lacks a comprehensive specification of input format and semantics, we have already established on the basis of the above rationale that our original PA predicates must be decomposed into simpler, primitive predicates that expose their inter-relations. For the purpose of the present discussion, we understand that it suffices to specify that our input will contain flat first-order logic-like conjunctions such as

$$\exists x\,(dance(x) \wedge female(x) \wedge human(x))\,,$$

in order to characterize entities, even if the final accepted language is sure to have a stricter logic component than first-order logic and might involve crossings with yet other formalisms. Predicates, fortunately, are not necessarily unary; and, for example, "A ballerina tapped a lovely she-dog" might well be generated from the following input:

$$\exists e, x, y \begin{pmatrix} dance(x) \wedge female(x) \wedge \\ \wedge human(x) \wedge event(e) \wedge \\ \wedge\, past(e) \wedge tap(e,x,y) \wedge \\ \wedge female(y) \wedge dog(y) \wedge \\ lovely(y) \end{pmatrix}. \quad (1)$$

Deletion as the substance of disjunction. Naturally, simply creating one node for each input semantic literal is not at all the idea behind our model. For example, if "woman" is to be actually employed in a specific lexicalization task, then it should continue figuring as one single node in XDG analyses as usual in spite of potentially covering a complex of literals. In fact, XDG and, in specific, PA analyses should behave and resemble much the same as they used to.

However, one remarkable difference of analyses in our generation model as compared to parsing lies in the role and scope of deletion, which indeed constitutes the very substance of disjunction now. By assigning all nodes but the root one extra lexical entry synchronizing deletion on all dimensions[2], we build an unrestrained form of disjunction whereby whole sets of nodes may as well act as if not taking part in the solution. Now it is possible to create nodes at will, even one for each applicable lexical item, and rely on the fact that, many ill-formed outputs as the set of all solutions may contain, it still covers all correct paraphrases, i.e. those in which all and only the right nodes have been deleted. For example, should one node be created for each of "ballerina", "woman", "dancer", "dancing", "female" and "person", all possible combinations of these words, including the correct ones, are sure to be generated.

Our design obviously needs further constraining, yet the general picture should be visible by now that we really intend to finish model creation — or rather, start search — with (i) a bunch of perfectly floating nodes in that not one edge is given at this time, all of which are equally willing and often going to be deleted, and (ii) a bunch of constraints to rule out ill-formed output and provide for efficiency. There are two main gaps in this summary, namely:

- what these constraints are and
- how exactly nodes are to be created.

This paper restricts itself to the first question. The second one involves issues beyond lexicalization, actually permeating all generation tasks, and is currently our research priority. Consequently, in all our experiments most of model creation was handcrafted.

In the name of clarity, we shall hereafter abstract over deletion, that is to say we shall in all respects adhere to the illusion of deletion, that nodes may cease to exist. In specific, whenever we refer to the sisters, daughters and mothers of a node, we mean those not due to deletion. In other words, all happens as if deleted nodes had no relation whatsoever to any other node. This abstraction is extremely helpful and is actually employed in our implementation, as shown in Section 4.

[2]That is, specifying valencies such that an incoming *del* edge is required on all dimensions simultaneously.

3.1 How Nodes Relate

In the following description, we shall mostly restrict ourselves to what is novel in our model as compared to current practice in XDG modelling. Therefore, we shall emphasize dimension PA and the new constraints we had to introduce in order to have only the desired PA analyses emerge. Except for sparse remarks on dimension DS and its relationship with PA, which we shall also discuss briefly, we assume without further mention the concurrence of other XDG dimensions, principles and concepts (e.g. lexical synchronization) in any actual application of our model.

Referents, arguments and so nodes meet. For the most part, ruling out ill-formed output concerns posing constraints on acceptable edges, especially when one takes into account that all we have is some floating nodes to start with. Let us first recall that dimension PA is all about predicate arguments, which are necessarily variables thanks to the flat nature of our input semantics. Roughly speaking, each PA edge relates a predicate with one of its arguments and thus "is about" one single variable. Therefore, our first concern must be to ensure that every PA edge should land on a node that "is (also) about" the same variable as the edge itself.

In order to provide for such an "aboutness" agreement, so to speak, one must first provide for "aboutness" itself. Thus, we postulate that every node should now have two new features, namely (i) $hook$, identifying the **referent** of the node, i.e. the variable it is about, and (ii) $holes$, mapping every PA edge label ℓ into the **argument** (a variable) every possible ℓ-labelled outgoing edge should be about. Normally these features should be lexicalized. The coincidence with Copestake et al.'s terminology (Copestake et al., 2001) is not casual; in fact, our formulation can be regarded as a decoupled fragment of theirs, since neither our $holes$ involves syntactic labels nor are scopal issues ever touched. As usual in XDG, we leave it for other modules such as mentioned in the previous section to take charge of scope and the relationship between semantic arguments and syntactic roles. The role of these new features is depicted in Figure 3, in which an arrow does not mean an edge but the possibility of establishing edges.

Completeness and compositionality. Next we proceed to ensure completeness, i.e. that every so-

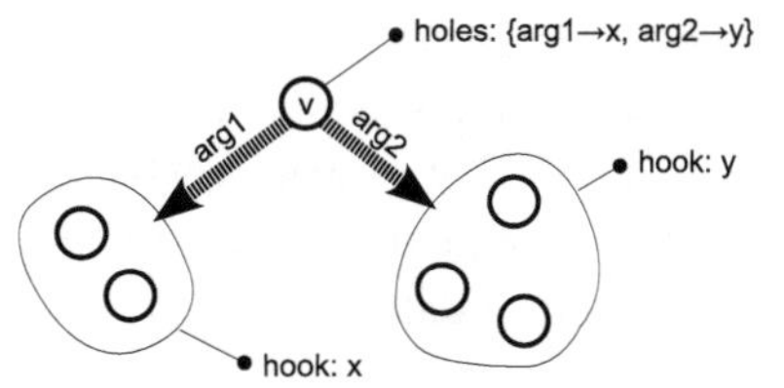

Figure 3: For every node v and on top of e.g. valency constraints, features $hook$ and $holes$ further constrain the set of nodes *able to receive* edges from v for each specific edge label.

lution should convey the whole intended semantic content. To this end, nodes must have features holding semantic information, the most basic of which is $bsem$, standing for *base semantic content*, or rather, the semantic contribution a lexical entry may make on its own to the whole. For example, "woman" might be said to contribute $\lambda x. female(x) \wedge human(x)$, while "female", only $\lambda x.\ female(x)$. Normally $bsem$ should be lexicalized.

In addition, we postulate feature sem for holding the **actual semantic content** of nodes, which should not be lexicalized, but rather calculated by a principle imposing **semantic compositionality**. In our rather straightforward formulation, for every node v, $sem(v)$ is but the conjunction of $bsem(v)$ and the sems of all its PA daughters thus:

$$sem(v) \\ = \\ bsem(v) \wedge \bigwedge \{sem(u) : v \to_{PA} u\}, \tag{2}$$

where $v \xrightarrow{\ell}_D u$ denotes that node u is a daughter of v on dimension D through an edge labelled ℓ (the absence of the label just denotes that it does not matter).

Finally, completeness is imposed by means of node feature $axiom$, upon which holds the invariant

$$sem(v) \Rightarrow axiom(v), \tag{3}$$

for every node v. The idea is to have $axiom$ as a lexicalized feature and consistently assign it the neutralizing constant $true$ for all lexical entries but those meant for the root node, in which case the value should equal the intended semantic content.

Coreference classes, concentrators and revisions to dimensions PA and DS. The unavoidable impediment to propagation is intrinsic choice, i.e. that between things equivalent and that we wish to remain so. That is exactly what we would like to capture for lexicalization while attempting to make the greatest amount of determinacy available to minimize failure. To this end, our strategy is to make PA analyses as flat as possible, with **coreferent nodes** — i.e. having the same referent or $hook$ — organizing in plexuses around, or rather, *directly below* hopefully one single node per plexus, thus said to be a **concentrator**. This offers advantages such as the following:

1. the number of leaf nodes is maximized, whose sem features are determinate and equals their respective $bsems$;

2. coreferent nodes tend to be either potential sisters below a concentrator or deleted. This allows most constraints to be stated in terms of direct relationships of mother-, daughter- or sisterhood. Such proximity and concentration is rather opportune because we are dealing simply with *potential* relationships as nodes will usually be deleted. In other words, our constraints aim mostly at ruling out undesired relations rather than establishing correct ones. The latter must remain a matter of choice.

It is in order to define which are the best candidates for concentrators. Having different concentrators in equivalent alternative realizations, such as "a ballerina", "a female dancer" or "a dancing woman" (hypothetical concentrators are underlined), would be rather hampering, since the task of assigning "concentratingness" would then be fatally bound to lexicalization disjunction itself and not much determinacy could possibly be derived ahead of committing to this or that realization. In face of that, the natural candidate must be something that remains constant all along, namely the *article*. Certainly, what specific article and, among others, whether to generate a definite/anaphoric or indefinite/first-time referring expression is also a matter of choice, but not pertaining to lexicalization. For the sake of simplicity and scope, let us stick to the case of indefinite articles, keeping in mind that possible extensions to our model to cope with (especially definite anaphoric) referring expression generation shall certainly require some revisions.

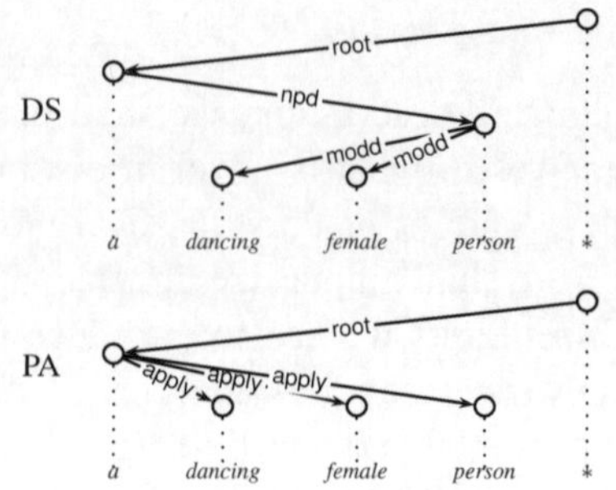

Figure 4: new PA and DS analyses for "a dancing female person". An asterisk stands for the root node

Electing articles for concentrators means that they now *directly* dominate their respective nouns and accompanying modifiers on dimension PA as shown in Figure 4 for "a dancing female person". One new edge label $apply$ is postulated to connect concentrators with their complements, the following invariants holding:

1. for every node v, $hook(v) = holes(v)(apply)$, i.e. only coreferent nodes are linked by $apply$ edges;

2. every concentrator lexical entry provides a valency allowing any number of outgoing $apply$ edges, though requiring at least one.

Roughly speaking, the intuition behind this new PA design is that the occurrence of a lexical (as opposed to grammatical) word corresponds to the evaluation of a lambda expression, resulting in a fresh *unary* predicate built from the $basesem$ of the word/node and the $sems$ of its children. In turn, every $apply$ edge denotes the application of one such predicate to the variable/referent of a concentrator. In fact, even verbs might be treated analogously if *Infl* constituents were modelled, constituting the concentrators of verb base forms. Also useful is the intuition that PA abstracts over most morphosyntactic oppositions, such as that between nouns and adjectives, which figure as equals there. The subordination of the latter word class to the former becomes a strictly syntactic phenomenon or, in any case, other dimensions' affairs.

Dimension DS is all about such oppositions, however, and should remain much the same except that the design is rather simplified if DS maintains concentrator dominance. As a result, articles must stand as heads of noun — or rather, de-

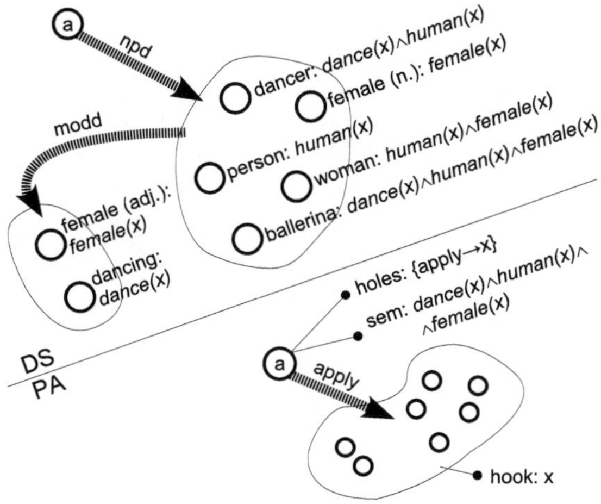

Figure 5: Starting conditions with perfectly floating nodes in the lexicalization of "a ballerina" and its paraphrases

terminer — phrases, which is not an unheard-of approach, just unprecedented in XDG. Naturally, standard syntactic structures should appear below determiners, as exemplified in Figure 4. Granted this, the flatness of PA and its relation to DS can straightforwardly be accomplished by the application of XDK library principles *Climbing*, whereby PA is constrained to be a flattening of DS, and *Barriers*, whereby concentrators are set as obstacles to climbing by means of special lexical features. Figure 5 thus illustrates the starting conditions for the lexicalization of "a ballerina" and its paraphrases, including the $bsems$ of nodes. Notice that we have created distinct nodes for different parts of speech of one same word, "female". The relevance of this measure shall be clarified along this section as we develop this example.

Fighting over-redundancy. We currently employ two constraints to avoid over-redundancy. The first is complete in that its declarative semantics already sums up all we desire to express in that matter, while the other is redundant, incomplete, but supplied to improve propagation.

The complete constraint is imposed between every node and each of its potential daughters. Apart from overhead reasons, it might as well be imposed between every pair of nodes. However, the set of potential daughters of a node v is best approximated by function $dcands$ thus:

$$dcands(v) = \left(\bigcup\{\langle x\rangle : x \in ran(holes(v))\}\right) - \{v\},$$

where $\langle x\rangle$ denotes the coreference class of variable x; and $ran(f)$, the range of function f. It is worth noticing that in generation $dcands$ is known at model creation.

Given a node u and a potential daughter $v \in dcands(u)$, this constraint involves hypothesizing what the actual semantic content of u would be like if v were *not* among its daughters. Let $hds_v(u)$ and $hsem_v(u)$ be respectively the hypothetical set of daughters of u counting v out and its "actual" semantic content in that case, which can be defined thus:

$$hds_v(u) = \{w : u \rightarrow_{PA} w\} - \{v\}$$

and

$$\begin{aligned} hsem_v(u) = bsem(u) \wedge \\ \wedge \bigwedge\{sem(w) : w \in hds_v(u)\}. \end{aligned} \tag{4}$$

The constraint consists of ensuring that, if the *actual* semantic content of the potential daughter v would be subsumed by the *hypothetical* semantic content of u, then v can never be a daughter of u. In other words, each daughter of u must make a difference. Formally, we have the following:

$$(hsem_v(u) \Rightarrow sem(v)) \rightarrow \neg(u \rightarrow_{PA} v) \tag{5}$$

where the two implication symbols, $\Rightarrow$ and $\rightarrow$ have the same interpretation in this logic statement, but are nonetheless distinguished because their implementations are radically different as shall be discussed in Section 4. Constraint (5) is especially active after some choices have been made. Suppose, in our "a ballerina" example, that "dancing" is the only word selected so far for lexicalization. Let u and v be respectively the nodes for "a" and "dancing". In this case, the consequent in (5) is false and so must be the antecedent $hsem_v(u) \Rightarrow dance(x)$, which implies that $hsem_v(u)$ can never "contain" the literal $dance(x)$. From (4) and the fact that articles have neutral base semantics — i.e. $bsem(u) = true$ — it follows that all further daughters of u must not imply $dance(x)$. As that does not hold for "ballerina" and "dancer", these nodes are ruled out as daughters of u and thus deleted for lack of mothers. Conversely, if "ballerina" had been selected in the first place, (5) would trivially detect the redundancy of all other words and analogously entail their deletion.

In turn, the redundant constraint ensures that, for every pair of coreferent nodes u and $v \in \langle upvar(u) \rangle$, if the actual semantic content of v is subsumed by u, then they can never be *sisters*. Formally:

$$\begin{array}{c}(sem(u) \Rightarrow sem(v)) \rightarrow \\ (v \notin sisters_{PA}(u))\,.\end{array} \quad (6)$$

This constraint is remarkable for being active even in the absence of choice since it is established between potential sisters, which usually have their $sems$ sufficiently, if not completely, determined. Surprisingly enough, the main effect of (6) is on syntax, by constraining alliances on DS. As our new version of the XDK's *Climbing* principle is now aware of sisterhood constraints, it will constrain every node on PA to have as a mother on DS either its current PA mother or some node belonging to one of its PA sister trees[3]. In ground terms, when (6) detects that e.g. "woman" subsumes "female (adj./n.)" and constrains them not to be sisters on PA, the *Climbing* principle will rule out "woman" as a potential DS mother of "female (adj.)". It is worth mentioning that once $v \notin sisters_D(u)$ is imposed, our sisterhood constraints entail $u \notin sisters_D(v)$.

Redundant compositionality constraints. Although a complete statement of semantic compositionality is given by Equation 2, we introduce two redundant constraints to improve propagation. The first of them attempts to advance detection of nodes whose semantic contribution is strictly required even before the sem features of their mothers become sufficiently constrained. It does so by means of an strategy analogous to that of (5), namely by hypothesizing, for every node v, what the *total* semantic content would be like if v were deleted. Let $root$, $hdown_v(u)$ and $htotsem_v$ be respectively the root node, the set of nodes directly or indirectly below u counting v out, and the total semantic content supposing v is deleted, which can be defined thus:

$$hdown_v(u) = down_{PA}(u) - \{v\}$$

and

$$htotsem_v = \bigwedge \{sem(u) : u \in hdown_v(root)\}\,.$$

[3]If the *subgraphs* option is active, which is the case here.

The constraint can be formally expressed thus:

$$deleted(v) \rightarrow (htotsem_v \Rightarrow sem(v))\,. \quad (7)$$

Unfortunately, (7) is not of much use in our current example, better applying to cases where there are a greater number of alternative inner nodes. For example, in the lexicalization of (1), this constraint was immediately able to infer that "lovely" must not be deleted since it was the sole node contributing $lovely(y)$.

The second redundant compositionality constraint attempts to advance detection of nodes not counting on enough potential sisters to fulfill the actual semantic content of their mothers. To this end, for every node v, the following constraint is imposed:

$$\begin{array}{c}\bigwedge \{sem(u) : u \rightarrow_{PA} v\} \\ = \\ \left(\begin{array}{c}\bigwedge \{bsem(u) : u \rightarrow_{PA} v\} \\ \wedge \\ \bigwedge \{sem(u) : u \in eqsis_{PA}(v)\}\end{array}\right),\end{array} \quad (8)$$

where

$$eqsis_D(v) = \left\{\begin{array}{l}\emptyset, \text{ iff } v \text{ is deleted on } D \\ sisters_D(v) \cup \{v\}\,, \text{ else.}\end{array}\right. \quad (9)$$

which reads "the actual semantic content of the mothers of a node is equal to their base semantic content in conjunction with the actual semantic content of this node and its sisters". It is worth noticing that, when v is deleted, both $\{u : u \rightarrow_{PA} v\}$ and $eqsis_{PA}(v)$ become empty so that (8) still holds. This constraint is especially interesting because our new versions of principles *Climbing* and *Barriers*, which hold between DS and PA, propagate $sisters$ constraints in both directions. In association with (6) and (8), these principles promote an interesting interplay between syntax and semantics. Resuming our example, let v be node "female (n.)". Before any selection is performed, constraint (6) infers that only "dancing", "person" and "dancer" can be sisters to v on PA and thus (now due to *Climbing*) daughters to v on DS. They cannot be mothers to v because its valency on DS and *Climbing* are enough to establish that, if v has any mother at all on DS, it is "a". Again taking the DS valency of v into account, it is possible to infer that, if v has any daughter at all on DS, it is "dancing", i.e. the only adjective in the original set of candidate daughters. It is the new sisterhood-aware version of *Barriers* that propagates this new piece of information back to PA. This principle now knows that the sisters of v on PA must come from either (i) the tree below v on DS, (ii) one of its DS sister trees or (iii) some DS tree whose root belongs to $eqsis_{DS}(inter)$ for some node $inter$ appearing — on DS — between v and one of its mothers on PA. In our example, (ii) and (iii) are known to be empty sets, while (i) is at most "dancing". Consequently, "dancing" is the only potential PA sister of v. Now (8) is finally able to contribute. As "a" is the only possible DS mother of v and any article has empty basic semantics, one is entitled to equate $\bigwedge \{sem(u) : u \rightarrow_{PA} v\}$ to $\bigwedge \{sem(u) : u \in eqsis_{PA}(v)\}$. Even though it is not known whether v will ever have mothers or daughters, (8) knows that the left-hand side of the equation yields either the whole intended semantics or nothing, while the right-hand side yields either nothing or at most $dance(x) \wedge female(x)$. Therefore, the only solution to the equation is nothing on both sides, implying that $eqsis_{PA}(v)$ is empty and thus v is deleted by definition (9).

Such strong interplay is only possible because we have created distinct nodes for the different parts of speech — or rather, the two different DS valencies — of "female". With somewhat more complicated, heavier constraints it would be possible to have the same propagation for one single node selecting from different parts of speech. Notwithstanding, that does not seem worth the effort because a model creation algorithm would be perfectly able to detect the diverging DS valencies, create as many nodes as needed and distribute the right lexical entries among them.

4 Implementation and Performance Remarks

The ideas presented in Section 3 were fully implemented in a development branch of the XDK. As with the original XDK, all development is based on the multiparadigm programming system Mozart[4].

The implementation closely follows the original CP approach of the XDK and strongly reflects the constraints we have presented after some rather standard transformations to CP, namely:

- variable identifiers in *hook*s and *holes*, as well as all semantic input literals such as $human(x)$ and $tap(e, x, y)$, are encoded as integer values. Features *bsem*/*sem* are implemented as set constants/variables of such integers;
- logic conjunction $\wedge$ is thus modelled by set union $\cup$. Each "big" conjunction is reduced to the form $\bigwedge \{f(v) : v \in V\}$, where V is a set variable of integer-encoded node identifiers, and modelled by a *union selection constraint* $\bigcup \langle f(1)\ f(2) \ldots f(M)\rangle\,[V]$, where M is the maximum node identifier and which constrains its result — a set variable — to be the union of $f(v)$ for all $v \in V$;
- implications of the form $x \Rightarrow y$ are implemented as $y \subseteq x$, while those of the form $x \rightarrow y$ as $reify(x) \leq reify(y)$, where the result of $reify(x)$ is an integer-encoded boolean variable constrained to coincide with the truth-value of expression x.

Our branch of the XDK now counts on two new principles, namely *(i) Delete*, which requires the *Graph* principle, creates doubles for the node attributes introduced by the latter, providing the illusion of deletion, and introduces features for sisterhood constraints; and *(ii) Compsem*, imposing all constraints described in Section 3.

A few preliminary proof-of-concept experiments were carried out with input similar to (1) and linguistically and combinatorially analogous to our "ballerina" example. In all of them, the system was able to generate all paraphrases with no failed state (backtracking) in search, which means that propagation was maximal for all cases. Although our design supports more complex linguistic constructs such as relative clauses and preposition phrases and is expected to behave similarly for those cases, we have not made any such experiments so far. This is so because we are currently prioritizing the issue of model creation and coverage of other generation tasks.

5 Conclusions and Future Work

In this paper we have presented the results of the very first steps towards the application of XDG to Natural Language Generation, hopefully in an integrated architecture. Our main contribution and focus was a formulation of lexicalization disjunction in XDG terms, preserving the good properties of modularity and extensibility while achieving

[4]http://www.mozart-oz.org

good propagation. We also hope to have demonstrated how strong the interplay between linguistic dimensions can be in XDG. As basic issues as the very nature of input were discussed also as an evidence that there is still a long way to go. We are currently working on extending our design to cover other generation tasks than lexicalization and perform model creation.

Acknowledgements

We would like to thank Claire Gardent and Denys Duchier, for all their invaluable insights and comments, and group Langue & Dialogue and Brazilian agencies CNPq and CAPES, for funding this research project and travel to COLING/ACL.

References

Copestake, A. A., Lascarides, A., and Flickinger, D. (2001). An algebra for semantic construction in constraint-based grammars. In *Meeting of the Association for Computational Linguistics*, pages 132–139.

Debusmann, R. (2004). Multiword expressions as dependency subgraphs. In *Proceedings of the ACL 2004 Workshop on Multiword Expressions: Integrating Processing*, Barcelona/ESP.

Debusmann, R., Duchier, D., Koller, A., Kuhlmann, M., Smolka, G., and Thater, S. (2004a). A relational syntax-semantics interface based on dependency grammar. In *Proceedings of the COLING 2004 Conference*, Geneva/SUI.

Debusmann, R., Duchier, D., and Kruijff, G.-J. M. (2004b). Extensible dependency grammar: A new methodology. In *Proceedings of the COLING 2004 Workshop on Recent Advances in Dependency Grammar*, Geneva/SUI.

Debusmann, R., Duchier, D., and Niehren, J. (2004c). The xdg grammar development kit. In *Proceedings of the MOZ04 Conference*, volume 3389 of *Lecture Notes in Computer Science*, pages 190–201, Charleroi/BEL. Springer.

Debusmann, R., Duchier, D., and Rossberg, A. (2005). Modular Grammar Design with Typed Parametric Principles. In *Proceedings of FG-MOL 2005*, Edinburgh/UK.

Debusmann, R. and Smolka, G. (2006). Multi-dimensional dependency grammar as multigraph description. In *Proceedings of FLAIRS-19*, Melbourne Beach/US. AAAI.

Reiter, E. and Dale, R. (2000). *Building Natural Language Generation Systems*. Cambridge University Press.

Van Roy, P. and Haridi, S. (2004). *Concepts, Techniques, and Models of Computer Programming*. MIT Press.

Author Index

Association for Computational Linguistics
209 N. Eighth Street
Stroudsburg, Pennsylvania 18360